INSIGHT GUIDES

BEIJING
Step by Step

D0227133

APA PUBLICATIONS
Part of the Langenscheidt Publishing Group

CONTENTS

Introduction

About this Book	4
Recommended Tours	6

Orientation

Overview	10
Food & Drink	14
Shopping	16
Entertainment	18
History: Key Dates	20

Walks and Tours

1. Imperial Beijing	24
2. Wangfujing and the Foreign Legation Quarter	32
3. Lama Temple, Confucius Temple and Ditan Park	38
4. The Lake District	42
5. Temple of Heaven	48
6. Tiananmen and Sanlitun at Night	51
7. Dazhalan & Liulichang	54
8. The Summer Palace	58
9. Beijing for Kids	61
10. Old and New Beijing	64
11. The Olympic Park	69
12. Modern Art	71
13. Fragrant Hills Park	75
14. The Ming Tombs and the Great Wall at Mutianyu	78
15. Cuandixia	84
16. Chengde	86

Directory

A–Z	92
Accommodation	106
Restaurants	112
Nightlife	118
Place Names in Chinese	122

Credits and Index

Picture Credits	124
Index	126

Above from top: the Great Wall at Mutianyu; boat cruise at the Summer Palace; National Stadium; exhibit at Beijing Tokyo Art Projects in 798 Art District; roof detail in Cuandixia village.

ABOUT THIS BOOK

This *Step by Step Guide* has been produced by the editors of Insight Guides, whose books have set the standard for visual travel guides since 1970. With top-quality photography and authoritative recommendations, this guidebook brings you the very best of Beijing in a series of 16 tailor-made tours.

WALKS AND TOURS

The tours in the book provide something to suit all budgets, tastes and trip lengths. As well as covering Beijing's classic attractions, of which there are myriad, the tours track lesser-known sights and up-and-coming areas; there are also excursions for those who want to extend their visit outside the city.

The tours embrace a range of interests, so whether you are an art enthusiast, a gourmet, a park lover, an architecture fan or have kids in tow, you will find an option to suit.

We recommend that you read the whole of a tour before setting out. This should help you to familiarise yourself with the tour and enable you to plan where to

stop for refreshments – options for this are shown in the 'Food and Drink' boxes, recognisable by the knife and fork sign.

For our pick of the walks by theme, consult Recommended Tours For… *(see pp.6–7)*.

ORIENTATION

The tours are placed in context by this introductory section, giving an overview of the city to set the scene, plus background information on food and drink, shopping and nightlife. A succinct history timeline in this chapter highlights the key events that have shaped Beijing over the centuries.

DIRECTORY

Also supporting the tours is the Directory chapter, comprising a user-friendly, clearly organised A-Z of practical information, our pick of where to stay while you are in the city and select restaurant listings; these eateries complement the more low-key cafés and restaurants that feature within the tours themselves and are intended to offer a wider choice for evening dining.

The Author

Eric Abrahamsen arrived in Beijing as a student in late 2001, and could not bring himself to leave after his studies concluded. He has worked as an editor at a local entertainment magazine, a freelance journalist and a writer and editor of all manner of texts. He is now primarily a literary translator, hoping that this will provide, if not a comprehensive picture of Chinese culture, at least a unique window onto it. Eric thinks walking is really the best way of getting to know Beijing.

The entire book has been thoroughly updated by David Drakeford, a freelance journalist and Insight regular who has lived and worked in Beijing for the past 6 years.

Margin Tips
Shopping tips, quirky anecdotes, historical facts and interesting snippets help visitors make the most of their time in Beijing.

Feature Boxes
Notable topics are highlighted in these special boxes.

Key Facts Box
This box gives details of the distance covered on the tour, plus an estimate of how long it should take. It also states where the route starts and finishes, and gives key travel information such as which days are best to do the tour or handy transport tips.

Route Map
Detailed cartography with the walk or tour clearly plotted using numbered dots. For more detailed mapping, see the pull-out map, which is slotted inside the back cover.

Footers
Those on the left-hand page give the tour name, plus, where relevant, a map reference; those on the right-hand page cite the main attraction on the double page.

Food and Drink
Recommendations of where to stop for refreshment are given in these boxes. The numbers prior to each café/restaurant name link to references in the main text. Places recommended en route are also plotted on the maps.

The $ signs given in each entry reflect the approximate cost of a two-course meal for one, with an alcoholic drink. These should be seen as a guide only. Price ranges, which are also quoted on the inside back flap for easy reference, are as follows:

$$$ over 200 yuan
$$ 100–200 yuan
$ 50–100 yuan

FAMILIES WITH KIDS

Beijing can be a welcoming place for those with kids. Try out aquariums, zoos and play spaces, or just hang out in one of the city's child-friendly parks (walk 9).

RECOMMENDED TOURS FOR...

OUTDOOR ENTHUSIASTS

See the Great Wall of China outside of Beijing (walk 14). Explore the hills closer to the city (walk 13) or climb up another for great vantage on an ancient Ming-era town (walk 15).

EARLY MORNING

Beijing rewards early risers. See *taiji* practice at the Temple of Heaven (walk 5) and watch residents swim in the Back Lakes (walk 4).

MODERN CULTURE

Immerse yourself in modern art at the 798 Art District (walk 12), or go for smaller, more select galleries near the Forbidden City (walk 6) or the museum at the Poly Plaza (walk 10).

GOOD WEATHER

A really beautiful day is a rare thing in Beijing, so make the most of it. Climb the Fragrant Hills (walk 13) or wander by the idyllic lakes that dot Beijing's centre (walk 4).

RELIGIOUS CENTRES

Buddhism is China's most deep-rooted religion, and the Lama Temple is the best spot to soak in that atmosphere (walk 3). Beijing is also home to a very old mosque (walk 7) and a number of lovely Catholic cathedrals (walk 2).

THE GRAND TOUR

Experience the grandeur of imperial Beijing. Start from Tiananmen Square, the heart of the nation, and proceed through the Forbidden City (walk 1). Hit the Temple of Heaven to see where emperors once worshipped the cosmos (walk 5), and the Ming Tombs to see a fitting end for a Son of Heaven (walk 14).

VIEWS OF PAST AND PRESENT

History is piled on Beijing in layers. Stroll through the Foreign Legation Quarter for remnants of the West's presence (walk 2); and walk through Dongsi to see old *hutong* neighbourhoods (walk 10). Then contrast old Beijing with the new CBD (walk 10) and the space-age Olympic facilities (walk 11).

FOOD AND DRINK

Beijing is home to some excellent cuisines, both foreign and local. Sample fine dining at The Courtyard (walk 6), eat like a Communist leader (walk 10) or an emperor (walk 4), or sample classic Beijing snacks (walk 6).

SHOPPING

Get your fill of modern articles at the Silk Market (walk 10), or head to Dazhalan and Liulichang (walk 7) for products you'll find only in Beijing.

ORIENTATION

An overview of Beijing's geography, culture and people, plus illuminating background information on food and drink, shopping, nightlife and history.

CITY OVERVIEW   10
FOOD AND DRINK   14
SHOPPING   16
ENTERTAINMENT   18
HISTORY: KEY DATES   20

CITY OVERVIEW

Apart from its blindingly obvious structures of unparallelled grandiosity, Beijing's greatest treasures are hidden, tucked into hutong (alleyways) and corners, best accessible through patient, on-the-ground exploration.

When to Visit

Winters are cold, dry and windy; summers are unrelentingly hot and muggy. It is best to go either in April/May or late September/October, when the skies are clear (apart from the spring sandstorms that blow in from the Gobi Desert) and strolling is a real pleasure.

The Beijing municipality covers 16,808 sq km (6,488 sq miles). To its south is the fertile North China Plain and to the east, the Bohai Sea. To the west, north-west and north-east are mountain ranges. Its location as the imperial seat of several dynasties, including the Liao, Jin, Yuan, Ming and Qing, was selected both for reasons of *feng shui* – mountains to the north and water or plains to the south are considered auspicious – and of defence – a series of mountain passes shield Beijing from the northern nomadic tribes.

CITY LAYOUT

At the heart of Beijing is the Forbidden City, which used to be the imperial palace and is now a gigantic open-air museum. To its south is the world's largest public square, the Tiananmen Square, where Communist buildings and monuments hold court. Immediately south of the square is an area of rapidly gentrifying *hutong* (alleyways), a tourist-friendly taste of old Beijing and its traditional businesses re-imagined for modern convenience.

To the Forbidden City's east is Wangfujing, Beijing's premier shopping street. Further east is the Chaoyang district, where international businesses, skyscrapers and expatriates gather. To the west and the north of the Forbidden City are the pretty back lakes, home to atmospheric *hutong*, bars and cafés.

The ancient plans of the imperial city still dictate the shape and flow of the modern capital, though not always in a positive way. The city wall of the Ming and Qing dynasties, demolished in the 1950s, defines Erhuan Lu (Second Ring Road), the primary artery of the city. The modernisation efforts of the past decades – arterials, Soviet-inspired ring roads, skyscrapers and overpasses – have not changed the city's essential layout.

Urban Sprawl

Beijing's roads (not to mention its air), designed long before the automobile, simply cannot handle the burden of a population enamoured with cars, especially when more than a thousand new vehicles are added to the roads each day. To make matters worse, the traditional city was made up of one- or two-storey buildings, none taller than the Forbidden City. This means the population density in the old city within the Second Ring Road is very low. Beijing has thus expanded outward into suburban sprawl, with endless forests of identical apartment buildings.

Traditional Beijing

Since the Yuan dynasty, established by the Mongolians, Beijingers have lived in single-storey homes with tile roofs, which face a central courtyard and are protected by high walls. These are set within a maze of *hutong*, some dating back many centuries and one of Beijing's most alluring sights.

One *hutong* area not to be missed is that around the Bell and Drum towers and the back lakes of the Forbidden City *(see p.43)*. Strolling or cycling around the area is a delightful experience. There are tiny workshops dimly lit by a single bulb, elderly men carrying their songbirds in cages, street vendors selling steaming buns – see these before they disappear.

NAVIGATING THE CITY

Moving through the city is relatively convenient apart from during morning and evening rush hours that can last several hours. Unfortunately, these affect both taxi and subway journeys though the extensive underground rail network and armies of patrolling taxis are still far and away the easiest ways to get around.

Though Beijing is ostensibly laid out on a grid, navigation is still tricky. The names of streets often change halfway, or differ from one another only by a single syllable. Sometimes they are marked with one name on the map, and referred to by another in speech.

North, South, Inside, Outside

North and south, inside and outside – these were crucial concepts to the planners of the old city. The Forbidden City had to have its back to the north and face south, laid out on a north–south axis. It may be worth learning the Chinese words for north, south, east and west (*bei, nan, dong* and *xi*, respectively), as many streets have mirror-image counterparts elsewhere, the result of a traditional love of symmetry. The concepts of *nei* and *wai* (inside and outside, respectively) once took the emperor's throne as the centre – now these terms most often refer to the inside or outside of Erhuan Lu, the Second Ring Road. Thus, Chaoyangmen Neidajie is the large street (*dajie*) that runs inside (*nei*) the Second Ring Road from Chaoyangmen Bridge, and Chaoyangmen Beixiaojie is the small street (*xiaojie*) that runs north (*bei*) from Chaoyangmen Neidajie.

Above from far left: the rotund Hall of Prayer of Good Harvests at the Temple of Heaven; heed the sign – be a good citizen; night out in Lotus Lane.

Below: the Bell Tower in the Lake District.

Above from left:
streetside pitstop for
tea and snacks;
a Beijinger's pet bird;
bicycles, bicycles
everywhere in Beijing.

Street numbers exist, but they are essentially useless for navigation. Taxi drivers will know the names of major streets, as well as the locations of overpasses, hotels, shopping malls and other landmarks.

Once on foot, you will find things are not necessarily easier. Sidewalks peter out unexpectedly, turn into parking lots or storefronts, or there are trees planted smack in their middle. Overpasses are sporadic. Many drivers completely disregard the rights of pedestrians, turning without warning or roaring through crosswalks with horns blaring. Walking in Beijing takes some getting used to – the best tactic is to stick to the centre of pedestrian herds.

Little Emperors

Since the one-child policy was introduced in 1979, a single child often has a monopoly over two doting parents and four grandparents. Memories of hard times and the desire to get the most out of one offspring mean many parents believe bigger is better. Obesity has become common among urban children puffed up by snacks, sweets and Western fast food. In return for the attention, the 'little emperors' face pressure to succeed in their examinations. Yet the sympathy is in short supply. 'Many of them are selfish, lazy, arrogant and uncaring', wrote *China Daily*.

BEIJINGERS

Beijing has a population of more than 19 million, making it China's second-largest city after Shanghai. Han Chinese make up about 96 percent of the population. As many as four million migrant workers from other parts of the country and around 90,000 foreigners live in Beijing.

Beijing residents have a unique reputation among Chinese from other parts of the country. As the seat of imperial power for a thousand years, Beijing cannot help but boast a certain historical status. True Beijing residents can often find royal blood in their family trees, or at least an association with the Banner Houses of the Qing dynasty. At the same time, Beijing's weighty political atmosphere has slowed its development in many ways. Compared with cities like Guangzhou or Shanghai, parts of the capital can appear behind the times, even frumpy – Shanghainese take a particular pleasure in calling Beijingers 'peasants'. The typical, traditional Beijing resident is gruff, plain-spoken and brooks no nonsense. The new generation of post-1980s and post-1990s urbanites, however, consider themselves to be living in a fully international city and take for granted everything that entails. They converse with friends via microblogs or over coffee at Starbucks, aspire to speak several languages, and seek individuality in their choice of clothing, musical taste and religion. Unsurprisingly, there is a yawning generation gap between these modern youngsters and parents whose jobs, housing and furniture may have been assigned to them by a work unit and who expect to have a say in almost every aspect of their children's lives.

It used to be that you could not tell rich Beijingers from poor, and lavishness was reserved for interiors only. This attitude is still reflected in the appearance of the streetsides and older suburbs that often seem unnecessarily run down. But duck behind a wall or go through a doorway, and an entirely new scene reveals itself. As Beijing becomes increasingly conscious of its status as a global capital, however, both the city and its people are beginning to change. An extraordinarily vast amount of money was spent on eye-catching modern architecture and a mass makeover of the city in the run-up to the 2008 Olympic Games, and house-proud residents and businesses have been beautifying their neighbourhoods since so as not to look bad by comparison.

CITY RHYTHMS

Beijing is awake and bustling by 7am. Even going out as early as 5.30am will reveal aspects of city life others never glimpse upon. If you visit the parks in the early morning or the lakes at twilight, you can get a sense of what city life used to be like. Twenty years ago, lights were out and the city was dead quiet by 8pm, but modern lifestyles are pushing bedtimes later and later, such that some neighbourhoods never sleep at all.

This early-rising tendency, combined with the remnants of an extraordinarily inefficient bureaucratic system, means that it is best to get official business done in the morning. Less modernised government offices are reluctant to do much of anything after 3pm. Massive (and seemingly unnecessary) quantities of paperwork are the norm as well, and it is usually a good idea to carry identification and official documents with you at all times.

Still, this is a far cry from the bad old days of the 1970s and 1980s, when shops displayed goods but refused to sell them, restaurant staff served customers if, and only if, they felt like it, and personal connections were needed to obtain a telephone line. The concepts of service and efficiency have gathered great strides in the private sector – and increasingly in the public sector, too.

Housing Headache
The cost of buying property in Beijing skyrocketed thanks to post-Olympic speculation. Out of reach for many ordinary people, getting onto the property ladder is now considered the number one hurdle for young couples looking to marry and set up a home.

Below: Beijing street scene.

FOOD AND DRINK

Eating is central to Chinese culture – it is the main activity of most celebratory occasions, the glue that holds families together and a necessary element in forging business and personal relationships. Small wonder, then, that one of Beijing's greatest riches is its restaurants.

Dining Etiquette
When you are invited into someone's home to eat, it is polite to bring a gift – alcohol or small presents typical of your home country. Take care of your neighbours at the table, serving them food from dishes that they can't reach easily. Don't pick out the best pieces in a dish, but take from the side closest to you.

The range of eating options in this city is enormous, from street vendors roasting sweet potatoes for a few yuan to Western restaurants dishing up meals with the high cost and service charge you'd expect to pay in London or New York. Thankfully for tourists, Beijing also offers cuisines from the country's various regions and from around the world at reasonable prices. In recent years, significantly fancier options have also been added – the worldwide cult of restaurants opened by personality chefs has finally come to the once-staid capital.

BEIJING AND REGIONAL CUISINES

Many dishes classified as Beijing-style actually originated from other parts of the kingdom, then perfected and embellished in the imperial court. Beijing cuisine makes liberal use of strong flavours from ingredients such as garlic, ginger, spring onion and coriander. Beijing's most famous traditional snack stalls live on at Jiumen Xiaochi, a well-known courtyard eatery that stands by Houhai lake. The vendors serve time-honoured culinary creations such as flash-boiled tripe, bean juice, wontons, sticky rice cakes and choice cuts from boiled sheep's head. The dishes of the north tend to be heartier, with noodles and steamed or fried bread, rather than rice, as the staple.

Diverse styles of the fancier 'imperial cuisine' are available in many restaurants around the city. The most common is the Manchu-Han Complete Feast *(manhan quanxi)*, which strives to replicate the dining habits and options of Qing-dynasty royalty, often Empress Dowager Cixi in particular. Other variations include Tan Family cuisine, favoured by a gourmand Qing official, and dishes inspired by those in Cao Xueqin's famous novel, *Dream of the Red Chamber*.

Jianbing, Beijing's most popular street snack, originated in Tianjin. It is a kind of pancake made with egg and spring onion, filled with crunchy, deep-fried dough sticks and garnished with chilli sauce and coriander. The most famous Beijing dish is Peking duck *(see p.15)*. Another popular meal, especially in winter, is Mongolian hot pot – slivers of mutton plunged into a trough of boiling water, fondue-style.

Beijing is also blessed with an excellent representation of food from all over the country. Favourite cuisines include Sichuan, Xinjiang (Uyghur), Yunnanese and Hunanese, and there is no shortage of Shaanxi noodle huts. Those in the know seek out provincial representative offices (*zhujing banshichu*, sort of mini-embassies belonging to each province), each of which has an attached restaurant serving that province's food.

Look around also for some weirder options – Cultural Revolution dining, North Korean food, and even dining in complete darkness in a restaurant with no lights.

PEKING DUCK

The earliest mention of Beijing's most famous dish, Peking duck, can be traced back to a 12th-century cookbook. Numerous restaurants in the city now serve this dish, but the most authentic spot to savour the bird is one of Quanjude's restaurants. The first Quanjude restaurant opened in 1864 in Qianmen *(see p.37)*.

To prepare the ambrosial Peking duck, the bird's unbroken skin is inflated like a balloon, filled with water and glazed with sugar. The duck is then roasted in an oven heated by burning the wood of fruit trees such as date, peach and pear. When the roast duck arrives, you fill your own pancakes at the table. Use your chopsticks to pick up some spring onion and use it as a kind of paint brush to dab a salty *hoisin* bean sauce on the pancake. Add one or two pieces of duck, roll the pancake and enjoy. Part of the art of this cuisine is to make use of the entire duck, and some restaurants claim to make more than 300 different duck dishes, to be sampled while the duck is being roasted. If you are adventurous, try dishes like the cold mustard duck web, deep-fried duck liver with sesame and fried duck hearts with chilli sauce.

DRINKS

Those hoping for local booze to match the food may be disappointed. The beer is weak, and China's greatest contribution to the pantheon of alcohols is 'white liquor' *(baijiu)*, best described as two-parts petrol, one-part French perfume. If you can find them, get a bottle of 'yellow liquor' *(huangjiu)* or rice wine *(mijiu)*, both far superior to their clear cousin. *Baijiu* is, unfortunately, a staple at business dinners, where drinking contests can influence the outcome of deals.

Above from far left: *lamian* noodle chef; bean curd dish; roasting Peking duck; selling braised meat and bean curd on the street.

Bottoms Up!
When your host makes a toast to you and says 'Ganbei!', meaning 'empty cup', you are obliged to empty your glass in one shot, and then turn your glass upside down to show that you've done it.

Below: dining at Quanjude restaurant.

SHOPPING

Growing affluence in Beijing means that for many, individualism now comes with a high price tag. New stores open almost every day. This is 'Socialism with Chinese characteristics', as the government calls it; 'unbridled consumerism' would be another way to put it.

International brands are aggressively expanding in Beijing, particularly in its gleaming new shopping developments. For local arts and crafts, the smaller streets and markets are still a better choice.

SPECIALITY MARKETS

Above: modern malls on Wangfujing shopping street.

The **Silk Market** (Xiushui Shichang; daily 9am–6pm) is located in a four-storey building at the Yong'anli subway stop. Its brand-name knock-offs are often targeted for intellectual property violation, but the 20,000 shoppers a day keep the store's doors open. Clothing, accessories, jackets and bags abound. **Yaxiu Market** (opposite the City Hotel, west of Sanlitun; daily 9.30am–8pm) is a popular alternative to the Silk Market. Both markets are great places to get cheap tailored clothing – just remember to knock more than half off the initial asking price.

There are several other good places to buy silk fabrics: **Yuan Long Silk Store** (north gate of the Temple of Heaven; daily 9am–6.30pm) and **Ruifuxiang Silk and Cotton Fabric Store** (Dazhalan Jie; daily 9am–7.30pm; *see p.55*).

Hongqiao Market (daily 8.30am–7pm), opposite the east gate of the Temple of Heaven on Tiantan Lu, has

Bargaining
Be stubborn but friendly, yet try not to appear too keen. Make your first offer no more than 50 percent of the shopkeeper's initial asking price. Be persistent, keep smiling and walk away if you find the price unacceptable.

antique clocks and Mao statues, as well as freshwater pearls and inexpensive reproduction antiques *(see p.50)*.

ANTIQUES/HANDICRAFTS

For antiques and traditional handicrafts, try **Liulichang** *(see p.56)* or the craft stores along **Guozijian Jie** *(see p.40)* or Nanluoguxiang. Further afield, but considered the most reliable source of collectables and memorabilia of all sorts, is **Panjiayuan Market** (Panjiayuan Jiuhuo Shichang; daily 7am–6.30pm, but it is best to go very early on a weekend morning) located just west of the Panjiayuan Bridge on the Dongsanhuan Donglu (East Third Ring Road). Much organised like a flea market, the outdoor stalls at Panjiayuan cover a large area and sell a large variety of objects, from reproduction ceramics to genuine antiques and curios, as well as Cultural Revolution-era posters and souvenirs and their reproductions. The weekend welcomes a large junk section with anything from plastic bathtubs to used bicycle bearings. Another place to look for curios is the **Beijing Antique City** (Beijing Guwancheng; daily 9.30am–6pm) at West Huawei Bridge, Dongsanhuan Nanlu (East Third Ring Road).

Note that it is illegal to export antiques that date from prior to 1795. Those that can be taken out of China must carry a small red seal or sticker, or have one affixed by the Cultural Relics Bureau. Beware of fakes: producing new 'antiques' (and the seal) is a thriving industry in China.

SHOPPING AREAS

Three lively shopping streets cater to Beijing's shoppers: **Wangfujing, Xidan** and **Dongdan**, all running north from Dongchang'an Jie. They offer inexpensive local goods from age-old Beijing brands, with clothing bargains. The **Beijing Painting & Calligraphy Store** (289 Wangfujing Dajie; daily 8.30am–7pm) has four floors of arts, crafts and jewellery. Further north, on the east side of Wangfujing is the **Foreign Languages Bookstore** (235 Wangfujing Dajie; daily 9am–9pm; see p.32), with a selection of novels and children's books in English.

Beijing's newest high-end shopping district is centred on the Sanlitun embassy district. Sanlitun Village draws crowds with flagship Adidas and Apple stores and clothes its shoppers with mid-priced labels such as American Apparel and The North Face. The newer and more luxurious Sanlitun Village North has luxury brand Emporio Armani and domestic designers Brand New China and Eldi. South of the village is Sanlitun SOHO, a mixed-use residential and commercial development that is filling up slowly with shops and fine restaurants.

SHOPPING MALLS

At the southern end of Wangfujing Dajie, opposite Beijing Hotel, is **Oriental Plaza** *(see p.32)*, the city's premier shopping venue – a vast complex with boutiques, restaurants and cafés. Further north up Wangfujing Dajie, **Sun Dong An Plaza**, also known as Xin Dong An, is another enormous, multi-tiered shopping mall.

The **Lufthansa Centre Youyi Shopping City** (52 Liangmaqiao Lu; daily 9am–9pm), another upmarket mall, carries products with a broader price range. It stocks one of Beijing's best selections of silk by the metre at reasonable prices.

Several other modern and fashionable malls have opened over the past few years in Beijing. The **Peninsula Arcade** (8 Jinyu Hutong; daily 9am–9pm) and the **China World Shopping Mall** (1 Jianguomenwai Dajie; daily 9am–9pm), both upmarket malls, are filled with international designer brands

Above from far left: contemporary art knock-offs; browsing in Panjiayuan Market; Communist memorabilia for sale.

Computer Products
For your computer-related needs, head to Haidian district's Zhongguancun, also known as Beijing's Silicon Valley, or if you're in the eastern part of the city, to Bainaohui on the south side of Chaoyangmenwai Dajie, across from Dongyue Temple.

Below: jewellery vendor in Panjiayuan Market

ENTERTAINMENT

In a short time, Beijing has gone from a staid city, where lights were out by 8pm, to a raucous party town. For a more subdued but no less vibrant experience, opt for performances of traditional opera or acrobatics.

Information
To keep up with what is going on in this fast-changing city, pick up free local English-language entertainment guides such as *That's Beijing*. Other regular publications include *City Weekend* and *Time Out*, available at hotels, restaurants and bars. Or check the following web listings: www.thats bj.com, www.city weekend.com.cn, www.xianzai.com.

If you want to do what most Beijingers do after the sun sets, the first place to go is where the food is: the night markets and restaurants. Night markets are fair-weather spots where you can sit outside, eat snacks and swill cool beer. If the weather is colder, seek out Mongolian hot pot, which epitomises the Chinese proverb of 'making one thing serve two purposes' by warming your hands as you cook your own dinner.

More 'formal' entertainments such as catching a show at a theatre are less popular with locals and it is usually the visiting foreign performers who create enough buzz to sell a decent amount of tickets. In recent years, several super-star performers of crosstalk – a type of comic dialogue that relies heavily on word-play – have emerged to fill houses, though the long-anticipated revival of Chinese performing arts has yet to be fully realised.

PEKING OPERA

Pop music may have captured the hearts of the masses, but there is a dedicated contingent of Peking opera fans who keep the art form alive. A word to the wise – if you're not yet sure if you like opera, go for the excerpts.

A sort of 'best of' Peking opera can be found at the Qianmen Hotel's

Liyuan Theatre (175 Yong'an Lu; performances daily 7.30–8.45pm; tel: 6301 6688, ext. 8860). Designed for foreign visitors, and using English subtitles, it tends to choose action-packed martial stories, as well as excerpts from the classic novel *Journey to the West*. These are great fun because the characters wear colourful costumes and there are plenty of acrobatics to dramatise battles.

More 'serious' locations include **Chang'an Grand Theatre** (7 Jianguomennei Dajie; tel: 6510 1310 ext. 10), Huguang Huiguan (3 Hufang Lu; tel: 6351 8284) and **Zhengyici Peking Opera Theatre** *(see p.56)*. Call in advance to check performance times.

ACROBATICS

The sad truth about acrobatics is that many of the big shows staged in Beijing follow the same staid routines that have been around for hundreds of years. It is rare, therefore, to meet locals who are keen to take in a show. The skill level of Chinese acrobats is beyond question, however, and many of the performances attract healthy numbers of tourists. You can catch a standard, kitschy Chinese show at the **Chaoyang Theatre** (36 Dongsanhuan Beilu; tel: 6506 0838; daily 8.30am–8.30pm), with plate-spinning, contortionists and 11 girls stacked onto a single bicycle.

Chinese martial arts have long played a part in performance. **Red Theatre** (44 Xingfu Dajie; tel: 135 5252 7373) puts on a nightly show 'The Legend of Kung Fu' combining acting, acrobatics and a performer showing off his kung fu skills through such feats as breaking a metal bar across his forehead.

THEATRE

Ticket prices at major theatres in Beijing are still out of reach of ordinary people, making the entertainment scene rather dominated by tourists and wealthy locals. Things are changing, however, and grass-roots performances now take place in areas that attract arty types – such as the Danshanzi Art District. Keen to make the controversial venue a success, the city government has been supporting the **National Centre for the Performing Arts** (Chang'an Avenue; tel: 6655 0000; www.chncpa.org) in its ability to attract big-name international acts. Another option is the **Capital Theatre** (22 Wangfujing Dajie; tel: 6524 9847; www.bjry.com), a large, Soviet-style building and a premier venue for Chinese-language theatre and occasional performance space for visiting troupes from abroad.

CONCERTS

The China Philharmonic Orchestra chooses the **Poly Theatre** (14 Dongzhimen Nandajie; tel: 6500 1188) for its concerts. You can also enjoy varied shows here performed by groups from around China and Asia. The China National Orchestra's regular venue is the **Beijing Concert Hall** (1 Beixinhua Jie; tel: 6605 5812).

NIGHTLIFE

Beijing's original bar street is Sanlitun Lu, where bars and clubs spill out in all directions including the Workers' Stadium area. Sanlitun is packed full of mediocre bars and untrained staff, so choose a reliable spot before you head out. Once-tranquil lake area Houhai has become a neon-lit free-for-all with a few nice spots. Chaoyang Park has many of the more expensive and, occasionally, classier venues. *For nightlife listings see pages 118–121.*

Above from far left: karaoke lounge; sign at Hard Rock Café, a live-music joint; Peking opera performer; bartender.

Tickets
Tickets for many cultural events in Beijing, including theatre, music, ballet and Peking opera, can be bought online from www.webtix.com.cn.

Below: a plate-twirling acrobatic performance.

HISTORY: KEY DATES

Beijing served as the capital of imperial dynasties for over 1,000 years.
After decades of turmoil under the Communists, the Deng era brought bold
market reforms, and the ensuing economic growth continues till this day.

EARLY HISTORY

1030–221 BC	The city of Ji develops on the site of Beijing.
221–207 BC	Emperor Qin Shi Huangdi unifies China.
200 BC–	Beijing becomes a strategic garrison town between warring
AD 1200	kingdoms.
1215	Mongols led by Genghis Khan overrun Beijing.

YUAN, MING AND QING DYNASTIES

1260	Kublai Khan founds the Yuan dynasty.
1271	Kublai Khan establishes the capital of Dadu (Khan Balik) in Beijing. Marco Polo visits China.
1368–1644	The Ming dynasty.
1400s	The Forbidden City and most of the existing Great Wall are built.
1644–1911	The Qing dynasty.
1839–42	The First Opium War.
1860	The Second Opium War.
1861–1908	Empress Dowager Cixi holds power.
1900	The Boxer Rebellion lays siege to the Foreign Legation Quarter.
1911	The revolution headed by Sun Yat-sen ends imperial rule.

Above: Emperor
Qianlong *(top)* and
Empress Dowager
Cixi *(bottom)* of the
Qing dynasty.

POST IMPERIAL CHINA

1919	The Treaty of Versailles cedes territory to Japan and sparks the May Fourth Movement for democracy and sovereignty.
1921	The Communist Party of China is founded in Shanghai.
1928	The Nationalist government establishes its capital in Nanjing.
1935	Communists embark on the Long March.
1937	Full-scale invasion by the Japanese, who occupy much of China until the end of World War II.
1949	Mao Zedong declares the People's Republic of China.
1957–59	Tiananmen Square and surrounding monoliths are built.

1957	The Anti-Rightist Movement singles out 300,000 intellectuals for criticism, punishment or imprisonment.
1958	Mao Zedong launches the disastrous Great Leap Forward.
1959–61	Great Leap Forward results in a famine that kills over 30 million.
1960	Beijing and Moscow split, beginning two decades of Cold War.
1966–76	The Cultural Revolution leads to widespread persecution, chaos and near economic collapse.
1972	President Nixon visits Beijing.
1976	Premier Zhou Enlai and Chairman Mao die.
1978	Premier Deng Xiaoping launches economic reforms.
1993	China's parliament officially endorses market economy and begins a series of structural reforms.
1997	Deng Xiaoping dies. Hong Kong returns to China. President Jiang Zemin consolidates power.
1999	China celebrates the 50th anniversary of its founding. Macau returns to China.

Above from far left: depiction of the Boxer Rebellion; the People's Liberation Army takes over Beijing in 1949.

21ST CENTURY

2001	China joins the World Trade Organization.
2003	Hu Jintao replaces Jiang Zemin as president; Wen Jiabao replaces Zhu Rongji as premier.
2008	The 29th Olympic Games are held in Beijing. China wins 51 gold medals. A $586 billion economic stimulus package for infrastructure and social welfare is announced to combat the global financial crisis.
2011	China overtakes Japan to become the world's second largest economy.

Above: key 20th- and 21st-century leaders: Mao Zedong (top); Deng Xiaoping (centre), Hu Jintao (bottom).

Left: Fuwa, the mascots of the Beijing Olympic Games, painted on souvenir porcelain plates.

WALKS AND TOURS

1. Imperial Beijing — 24
2. Wangfujing and the Foreign Legation Quarter — 32
3. Lama Temple, Confucius Temple and Ditan Park — 38
4. The Lake District — 42
5. Temple of Heaven — 48
6. Tiananmen and Sanlitun at Night — 51
7. Dazhalan and Liulichang — 54
8. The Summer Palace — 58
9. Beijing for Kids — 61
10. Old and New Beijing — 64
11. The Olympic Park — 69
12. Modern Art — 71
13. Fragrant Hills Park — 75
14. The Ming Tombs and the Great Wall at Mutianyu — 78
15. Cuandixia — 84
16. Chengde — 86

IMPERIAL BEIJING

First stop: the imperial heart of the city. See Beijing's most important sights, beginning with monumental Communist structures and the largest public square in the world before taking a tour of the Forbidden City. End the day relaxing in the gardens of Coal Hill Park.

Above:
Zhengyangmen, the main entrance to Tiananmen Square.

DISTANCE 3½km (2 miles)
TIME A full day
START Qianmen
END Coal Hill Park
POINTS TO NOTE

Be sure to bring water and some food, as it takes hours to see the Forbidden City in detail and there are few refreshment choices available inside. To reach the starting point of the tour, take the subway to the Qianmen stop. You can also reach Tiananmen by taking the subway to either the Tian'anmen Xi or Tian'anmen Dong stop.

For over half a millennium, the Forbidden City was the cradle of imperial politics and administration, while Tiananmen Square was where major

Below: Qianmen at night.

post-dynastic revolutionary events unfolded. Your first tour logically starts here at the heart of Beijing, where Chinese classical heritage and revolutionary symbolism converge.

SOUTH OF TIANANMEN SQUARE

Begin at **Qianmen** ❶ (Front Gate; daily 8.30am–4.30pm; charge), the largest of nine similar gates in the wall that used to embrace the Inner City, which has at its centre the Imperial Palace, also known as the Forbidden City. Qianmen, built in 1419, was initially used solely for the emperor's annual visits to the Temple of Heaven, where, after three days of fasting, he would pray for a good harvest. Residents outside the gate were forbidden to watch the procession, and had to keep their doors and windows sealed. Destroyed during the Boxer Rebellion of 1900, the gate was rebuilt in 1905. The front gate provides a great vantage point for studying the layout of old Beijing.

Qianmen is divided into two sections, which were once part of a single fortress-like complex. The northern section, across the street, is the main entrance of **Zhengyangmen** ('Facing the Sun' Gate), and the southern section is **Jianlou** (Arrow Tower), built in 1439 to serve as a watchtower. The Outer City, which was also enclosed by a high wall, extends southwards. Hard to ignore is the broad, pedestrianised shopping street Qianmen Dajie immediately south from which bustling, narrow streets to the south form the lively Dazhalan shopping district *(see p.55)*, which at the end of the 19th century teemed with decadent pleasures for off-duty officials. Further south is the Temple of Heaven *(see p.48)*.

Orientation

From Qianmen, you can get an overview of the imperial city. The north side of Qianmen overlooks Tiananmen Square, in the middle of which stands an obelisk, the Monument to the People's Heroes. To the left stands the Great Hall of the People, and to the right, the National Museum of China. In the centre of the square is the Mao Zedong Mausoleum.

At the far end of the square, across Dongchang'an Jie, is Tiananmen Gate, the Gate of Heavenly Peace, leading the way to the Forbidden City, which is now officially known as the Palace Museum (Gugong). To the immediate west of Tiananmen Gate is the entrance to Zhongshan Park, dedicated to the early Nationalist leader Sun Yatsen. The park used to be part of the Forbidden City, as did Zhongnanhai *(see p.46)* further west, where China's top leaders now live. To the north-west you can see the White Dagoba in Beihai Park *(see p.46)*, which was once part of the imperial gardens.

Before leaving Qianmen, visit the **photography exhibition** inside (daily 9am–4pm; charge). There are wonderful photographs of Beijing at the turn of the century, depicting scenes

Above from far left: facets of the Forbidden City: moat, Upright Gate and bronze urn; Tiananmen Gate.

Above: Monument to the People's Heroes.

from cricket fighting to camel caravans arriving at the city gate.

Mao Zedong Mausoleum

Join the queue to pay your respects at the **Mao Zedong Mausoleum** ❷ (Mao Zhuxi Jiniantang; Tue–Sun 8–11.30am, Aug–May also Tue, Thur 2–4pm; free), completed in 1977, a year after his death. Even today, when the little red book of Mao quotations is long past its sell-by date, people from all over China visit his mausoleum. You must leave your bag and camera at the door, or you will be turned away. Though the queue looks daunting, visitors are hustled through quickly. As you file past the Great Helmsman – one of the four Grand Old Men of Marxism-Leninism who are lying in state – you are likely to ponder the rumours of body doubles, nightly deep-freezes and parts falling off the Chairman. But also be aware of the reverence paid by those around you.

Just outside the mausoleum, you get a graphic picture of how socialism is fast becoming mere consumer kitsch, as people are ushered through a small bazaar selling Chairman Mao busts, bags, badges and musical lighters playing *The East is Red*.

Monument to the People's Heroes

The 37m (121ft) obelisk that you saw earlier in the centre of Tiananmen Square is called the **Monument to the People's Heroes** ❸ (Renmin Yingxiong Jinian Bei), dedicated in 1958 to those who died for the country. The bas-relief on the pedestal portrays the struggle from the First Opium War (1839–42) to the founding of the People's Republic of China (PRC) in 1949. Start on the east side and move clockwise to see it chronologically.

Great Hall of the People

Next, visit the **Great Hall of the People** ❹ (Renmin Dahuitang; daily 9am–5pm except during meetings; charge). Officially opened in 1959, this is where China's parliament, the National People's Congress, meets and other important conferences and diplo-

The Egg

For a glimpse of a new kind of national monument, walk around the northern end of the Great Hall of the People to the National Centre for the Performing Arts (Guojia Dajuyuan), formerly known as the China National Grand Theatre. This enormous edifice, disparagingly nicknamed 'The Egg', has been received with scepticism by most Beijing residents for being too grandiose, for ignoring the principles of *feng shui*, and for clashing with its surroundings. The grand theatre has since struggled to deliver high art to the masses or truly bring about a renaissance of the local Peking opera, though it is a popular spot for moat-side strolls (particularly when lit up at night) and an entrance ticket is an inexpensive way to marvel at its interior and view its exhibition areas.

diplomatic meetings take place. In the hall, there is one room dedicated to each of China's 32 provinces and regions. Across the square, another similarly imposing building houses the **National Museum of China** (Zhongguo Guojia Bowuguan; Tue–Sun 9am–5pm; free) which, following a four-year renovation, was opened in 2011 as the biggest museum in the world. A cavernous main hall is flanked by two wings boasting 65,000 sq m (700,000 sq ft) of exhibition space – one third of the entire floor area. Permanent exhibitions focus on Chinese arts, culture and, particularly, the long and tumultuous history of the world's oldest civilisation

here to demand that their government reform itself and the nation. Thirty years later on 1 October 1949, hundreds of thousands of cheering soldiers and citizens convened here to hear Mao Zedong declare the founding of the PRC from atop Tiananmen Gate. During the Cultural Revolution in the 1960s, Red Guards held their near-hysterical gatherings here, and there was a mass outpouring of grief in the square following the deaths of Zhou Enlai and Mao Zedong in 1976.

Today, Tiananmen Square is mostly packed with domestic tourists marvelling at the collection of extravagant monuments that form the centre of their

Above from far left: tourists and a guard outside the Mao Zedong Mausoleum; Socialist-style sculpture on Tiananmen Square; the grand Great Hall of the People.

Above: Tiananmen Square is one of the most popular tourist sights in Beijing.

TIANANMEN SQUARE

Take the opportunity to relax for a while in **Tian'anmen Guangchang** ❺ (Tiananmen Square). In the Ming and Qing times, two rows of ministry offices stood on this site. When the emperor wanted to hand down an edict, he would pass with great fanfare to deliver it to the Ministry of Rites, where it was recopied and distributed throughout the empire.

Many buildings in the square were demolished to make it larger than any other public square in the world, including Red Square in Moscow. For most Chinese, this area conjures up a wide range of images, both dark and joyous. Since the end of imperial times, the plaza has been at the heart of Chinese politics. In the spring of 1919, May Fourth protesters gathered

Food and Drink 🍴

① QUANJUDE

44 Dongjiaomin Xiang (south-eastern corner of Tiananmen Square); tel: 6512 2265; daily 11am–8pm; $$
Another branch of Beijing's most famous Peking duck outlet, this one is slightly more expensive than the others.

② DONGLAISHUN

44 Dongjiaomin Xiang (south-eastern corner of Tiananmen Square); tel: 6524 1042; daily 11am–8.30pm; $$
This hot-pot chain, first opened in 1903, is famous for the quality of its meat. *Shuanyangrou* is lamb dipped in boiling water, though in most restaurants the meat needs to be cooked for quite some time. Donglaishun's tender, thin sliced lamb, however, can literally be 'dipped' in the pot, then straight in the savoury sesame sauce. This is truly some of the best meat in the city.

Beneath the Square
A complex network of tunnels is rumoured to lie beneath the austere surface of Tiananmen Square. Built in the 1970s, the compound was intended to accommodate all of Beijing's inhabitants in the event of nuclear war.

Private City
Though more and more of the Forbidden City is open to the public, large tracts of it are still closed. Some areas serve as private residences for those working in the palace and (one suspects) government officials with a taste for history.

nation's great capital. A flag-raising and lowering ceremony is performed by PLA soldiers in the north of the square daily at sunrise and sunset *(see p.51)*.

Though this may be the centre of the city, the food situation here is sorely lacking. Besides streetside vendors, two restaurants, **Quanjude**, see 🍴①, *p.27*, and **Donglaishun**, see 🍴②, *p.27*, are practically the only choices. The smartest option may be to visit the Qianmen neighbourhood at the start of the day and stock up on local snacks for later. Don't forget bottled water. Save this food for the Forbidden City, which has only one, overpriced, café.

Zhongshan Park

If it is a warm day or if you are not up for the Forbidden City, **Zhongshan Park ❻** (Zhongshan Gongyuan; daily 6am–9pm; charge) makes for a lovely detour. Originally the Altar of Land and Grain, where the emperor would

Right: the Golden Water River (Jinshahe) flows in front of the Hall of Supreme Harmony.

pray and sacrifice for good harvests, it was made into a public park in 1914. The body of Sun Yat-sen (Sun Zhong-shan in Mandarin) was placed here briefly after his death in 1925, and from 1928 the park took his name. It now houses some exquisite botanical exhibitions and the Forbidden City Concert Hall, one of the best in the city.

Tiananmen Gate

After lunch, return to the **Tiananmen Gate ❼**, the Gate of Heavenly Peace (daily 8.30am–5pm; free to pass, charge to ascend), to enter the Forbidden City. The gate, built in 1417 and restored in 1651, was where emperors made their first offerings on their way from the Forbidden City to the Temple of Heaven for New Year rites. There are five passages through the massive gate walls, of which the central one follows the imperial route and was reserved for the emperor. Today, it is open to all.

Tiananmen Gate is now adorned with Mao's gigantic portrait and the slogans 'Long live the People's Republic of China' and 'Long live the great union of the peoples of the world'. It was here that Chairman Mao announced the founding of the PRC before a crowd of 300,000 in 1949.

FORBIDDEN CITY

From Tiananmen Gate, a long approach takes you through a second gate before reaching the **Forbidden City ❽** (Zijin Cheng; daily, Apr–Oct 8.30am–5pm, Nov–Mar 8.30am–4.30pm; charge), also called Imperial Palace or referred to by its official Chinese name of Palace Museum (Gugong). A useful and informative audio guide, available in eight languages, can be rented. The audio guide can be collected as you enter the Forbidden City through the glass doors to the right of the main entrance.

The approach to the Forbidden City has now become a bit of a circus, with vendors, souvenir photographers and people who insist on leading you to see their 'art gallery'. The latter typically approach in pairs, and try to take visitors to a nearby room where hasty sketches are sold at very high prices. Some of the flanking buildings do house sights of interest, however; the exhibitions of Qing-dynasty photographs are worth seeing.

History

Behind walls more than 10m (30ft) high and within the 50m (160ft) long moat, life in the palace was dictated by complex rules and rituals. Entrance was denied to ordinary people, but today's tourists can easily access this fascinating display of Chinese cultural history in what is probably the best-preserved site of classical Chinese architecture.

In 1421, after 17 years of construction, the Ming emperor Yongle moved into the palace. Up until the founding of the republic in 1911 – a period covering the reign of 24 emperors from the Ming dynasty until the last emperor of the Qing dynasty, Puyi – the Forbidden City was the imperial residence and the centre of the Middle Kingdom. It has 9,000 rooms in which an estimated 8,000 to 10,000 people lived, including 3,000 eunuchs, as well as maids and concubines, all within an area of 70 hectares (180 acres).

Layout and Palace Details

The entire site can be divided into two main areas: **Waichao**, the Outer Court in the south comprising three large halls where emperors held state cermonies; and **Neiting**, the Inner Residence in the rear, with three large palaces and a few smaller ones as well as the imperial gardens. Through the middle of the site runs the imperial walkway, which is decorated with finely carved stone phoenix and dragon bas reliefs, representing the empress and the emperor, respectively.

Among the details to look out for are

Above from far left: a large portrait of Chairman Mao graces the Tiananmen Gate; marching guards; tourists at the Forbidden City; palace architectural details.

Below: bronze lions guard the entrances to palace buildings.

Bored Figures
The stone creatures on roof corners figure in the Chinese saying *wuji liushou*, meaning 'as bored as the stone figures on the roof'.

the lion door guards, symbolising strength and dignity. On the right is usually a male lion pawing a ball, which is thought to represent the world. On the left, you often find a female with a cub under her paw. At the corners of most roofs are a parade of creatures often led by a man riding a hen. These were believed to discourage lightning from striking. Vast bronze urns are placed at regular intervals throughout the palace, and were once kept filled with water in case of fire, the greatest danger the palace faced.

Restoring the City

The Forbidden City lay abandoned until the mid 1980s. Protected by the army during the Cultural Revolution, it was largely ignored in the years after, in part due to a faint popular superstition that deterred 'commoners' from visiting the former Imperial Palace. Rare photos of the area depict a remarkable site of antiquity and decrepitude, with crumbled bricks and grass growing rampant in the courtyards. More recent repair projects have revived old building techniques. Wooden structures are built using mortise and tenon instead of nails, and paint is applied using silk rags, not brushes. A peculiar technique is also used to make the so-called 'gold bricks' and paving stones, such that when these bricks are struck, a metallic sound is produced.

Colours and numerology also have special significance. The yellow of the palace roof stands for the Earth; red walls represent fire, luck and happiness; blue and green mean spring and rebirth. Nine is a lucky number, reflected in the number of dragons on ramps and gold studs on doors.

Three Great Halls

Approaching from the **Meridian Gate** (Wumen), you see the three great halls and courtyards of the outer area. The **Hall of Supreme Harmony** (Taihedian) is the largest building in the palace, and also the first and most impressive of these. In its centre is the ornately carved golden **Dragon Throne**, from which the emperor ruled. Only he could enter the hall by walking up the ramp adorned with dragon motifs. On the platform in front of the hall are two symbols: a grain measure on the left and a sundial to the right, which represent agriculture and imperial justice, respectively. Solemn ceremonies, such as the enthronement of a new emperor, were held in this hall. The courtyard could hold 90,000 spectators.

The **Hall of Middle Harmony** (Zhonghedian) is behind the Hall of Supreme Harmony. This was where the emperor prepared for ceremonies before entering the main hall. On display here is an imperial palanquin. The **Hall of Preserving Harmony** (Baohedian) was used for examinations and lavish banquets. These two halls complete a trinity that reflects the Three Buddhas and the Three Pure Ones of Taoism. To the east of the Hall of Preserving Harmony is the magnificent **Nine Dragon Screen** (Jiulongbi).

Palace of Peace and Longevity
Facing the Nine Dragon Screen is the **Palace of Peace and Longevity** (Ningshougong). The last emperor Puyi lived in the palace until 1925, despite the founding of the republic in 1911. In 1932, he became the puppet emperor of Manchukuo, the Japanese-occupied territory in northeast China. Many palace treasures were stolen by the Japanese or taken to Taiwan by fleeing Nationalists, but the smaller halls to the east and the west of the main halls still contain the impressive collections of the Forbidden City. A highlight is the clock and jewellery hall, with water clocks and ornate mechanical clocks.

Palace of Heavenly Purity
On the other side of the imposing Outer Court, to the north and separated by the **Gate of Heavenly Purity** (Qianqingmen), lies a labyrinth of gates, doors, pavilions, gardens and palaces. This is called the **Palace of Heavenly Purity** (Qianqinggong), the residence of the imperial family, who were almost all exclusively female; the emperor and eunuchs were the only men permitted to enter. The male members of the emperor's family lived in prince's residences (*wangfu*, as in Wangfujing, *see p.32*) scattered around the city, which were generally palatial in their own right.

COAL HILL PARK

After dropping off your audio guide near the **Gate of the Divine Warrior** (Shenwumen), the north gate of the Imperial Palace, cross Jingshan Qianjie to **Coal Hill Park** (Jingshan Gongyuan; daily 6am–9pm; charge). This is the best place to appreciate the sheer scale of the palace complex, particularly at night when spotlights are trained on the corner towers. The artificial hill was built with the earth dug from the palace moats in the early 15th century. In Qing emperor Qianlong's day, the park was stocked with deer, rabbits and songbirds. The last Ming emperor, Chongzhen, fled the besieged Forbidden City and hanged himself from a tree on the hill in 1644. A new tree has been planted on the same spot to record the event for posterity.

Above from far left:
Meridian Gate; Palace of Peace and Longevity; Dragon Throne in the Hall of Supreme Harmony; Nine Dragon Screen.

Imperial Harem
Most of the women who lived in the Imperial Palace were chosen when they were very young girls. This brought great honour to their families, but once they were inside the palace walls, they never left again.

Below: springtime in Coal Hill Park.

WANGFUJING AND THE FOREIGN LEGATION QUARTER

Stroll through Beijing's main shopping street and then take a leisurely walk or cycle through the former Legation Quarter, a fascinating piece of preserved history where foreign diplomats lived at the turn of the last century.

DISTANCE 2½km (1½ miles)

TIME 2½ hours

START Oriental Plaza

END Beijing Hotel

POINTS TO NOTE

Take the subway to the Wangfujing stop, from where you can walk to Oriental Plaza.

The name Wangfujing dates back to the Yuan dynasty. Then it was called Wangfu Street, after a prince's resi-

dence that was located here. The name was changed later in the Ming dynasty when a well (*jing*) was discovered. By the late Qing dynasty the street was a major commercial thoroughfare and many of Beijing's age-old brand names can still be found here.

WANGFUJING STREET

At the southern end of **Wangfujing Dajie** (Wangfujing Street) is the vast **Oriental Plaza ❶** shopping complex, a mandatory shopping experience that is also home to one of Beijing's finest hotels, the **Grand Hyatt Beijing**. Peruse the complex at your leisure and then stroll north up Wangfujing Dajie, past the huge Wangfujing Bookstore, perhaps diving left into the **Wangfujing Xiaochijie** (Wangfujing Food Street). Marked by a decorated archway, this busy quarter teems with small restaurants and stalls serving dishes from all over China. About 100m/yds to the north, on the west side of the street, is the **Wangfujing Foreign Languages Bookstore** (tel: 8080 8383; daily 9.30am–4.30pm), one of the best spots in the city for books in English. While

Prince's Well

Though the prince's residence (*wangfu*) that gave the street its name is gone, the original location of the well (*jing*) is marked on the side of the street.

*Map labels:*

100 m / 110 yds

Nanheyan Dajie

Chenguang Jie

Dengshikou Dajie

Dongtang (St Joseph's Cathedral) ❷

DONGCHENG

Xitangzi Hutong

Jinyu Hutong

Wangfujing Foreign Languages Bookstore

Xin Dong An (Sun Dong An Plaza)

Wangfujing Dajie

Dongdan Beidajie

Mishitang (Rice Market Church)

Wangfujing Bookstore

Grand Hyatt Beijing

Beijing Hotel

Oriental Plaza ❶

Dongchang'an Jie

WANGFUJING

DONGDAN

FOREIGN LEGATION QUARTER

Taijichang Dajie

Chongwenmennei Dajie

see map opposite

CHONGWENMEN

the prices are comparable to what you would pay in a bookstore in America or Europe, the selection is fantastic.

ST JOSEPH'S CATHEDRAL

Head north 500m/yds to one of Beijing's most recognisable Catholic monuments, **St Joseph's Cathedral** ❷ (Dongtang). St Joseph's was originally built in 1655 by the Qing emperor Shunzhi for resident Jesuits, and has since symbolised the presence of the West in China under many different circumstances. It was damaged or destroyed countless times over the past few centuries – by earthquake in 1720, fire in 1812 and the Boxer Rebellion in 1900. It now serves an active congregation of foreign and Chinese worshippers. It is also a favourite setting for newly-weds and wedding photographers: its grand exterior and flocks of pigeons create the perfect atmosphere for brides and grooms looking for a sense of Europe. On nice days, three or four couples can be seen vying for good spots.

FOREIGN LEGATION QUARTER

Early 20th-century European architecture in China is an instant reminder of the ignominious decline of the Qing dynasty and the foreign domination that followed. The **Foreign Legation Quarter**, south of Oriental Plaza and east of Tiananmen Square, contains many elegant European buildings that recall part of modern China's history. Between the 1860s and the outbreak of the Sino–Japanese War in 1937, 13 foreign governments were represented here, their presence forced on the Chinese by the outcome of the Opium

Above from far left: bustling crowd on Wangfujing Food Street; roasted chestnuts for sale; Oriental Plaza; night-time Wangfujing shopping street.

Scams
Wangfujing is a prime spot for scams and sales pitches aimed at foreigners, usually beginning with two cheerful girls saying 'Nice to meet you!' Be friendly, but firm

Catholic Churches
None of the Catholic churches in China, including St Joseph's Cathedral *(above)*, are recognised by the Vatican.

Wars. They had their own administration, police, churches, hospitals, shops and post office, guarded by some 1,000 soldiers. In 1900, during the Boxer Rebellion, which was raging over much of northern China, the Foreign Legation Quarter was a main target. The area was shelled for a month or more, much of it flattened in the process. After the rebellion was put down, in part by foreign armies, diplomats more or less had a free hand exacting revenge on the former Boxers. Furthermore, the legation quarter was rebuilt and fortified with its own version of a city wall, and closed off to Chinese nationals.

Former Italian Legation

To get to the Foreign Legation Quarter, backtrack south to Oriental Plaza, cross over Dongchang'an Jie and head down Taijichang Dajie (Customs Street). About 200m/yds along on the right, at No. 1, you come to the gate of the **former Italian Legation ❸**, where the Italians relocated to in 1900 after the Boxer rebels destroyed their previous quarters. It now houses the Chinese People's Association for Friendship with Foreign Countries (CPAFFC).

Former Hungarian Legation

Continue along Taijichang Dajie but cross to the opposite side. Walk alongside a high grey wall topped with curved tiles and turn left into the first alleyway. About 200m/yds on the left is the **former Hungarian Legation ❹**, which is now the Institute of International Studies. Built in 1900, the simple grey-and-white building changed hands many times. In 1915, when China declared war on Germany and its allies, the building was occupied by the Hungarians. After a short spell under the Dutch, a Russian general turned it into a guesthouse in the late 1920s. In 1938, it became the German Club. The Americans used it for the Allied Property Administration and it later became the Hungarian Embassy. The building was finally returned to the Chinese in 1969.

Double back to Taijichang Dajie and

Diplomats' Haven

The establishment of the Foreign Legation Quarter was a long and drawn-out battle. The Qing government originally gave the diplomats a camp far outside the city walls. The Europeans protested and, after lengthy negotiations, were given the present location of the legation quarter. They congratulated themselves on their resounding success – being given a spot so close to the imperial palace had to be a sign of respect. What they did not know was that this was historically where barbarian chiefs from the north were housed, thus placing the foreigners in a distinctly disreputable tradition. They also did not know that present-day Zhengyi Lu, then a deep canal, was essentially the sewage outflow for the entire Forbidden City. They discovered their error, but no amount of petitioning could change the situation.

turn left. Through the first gate on the left is an elegant grey-blue building with arches along the ground floor, topped by a red national emblem and a single portal. This is the headquarters of the **Beijing People's Congress** (closed to the public). Built in 1902, it was once the Peking Club, with a swimming pool and tennis courts that were still in use as late as the 1960s. The white building opposite, topped with an enormous red star, is the headquarters of the Communist Party Committee of the Beijing municipality.

Former French Legation

Moving along Taijichang Dajie, you enter 'Little France'. The French, along with the British, were the first to install permanent diplomatic representatives here. They held large tracts of land on both sides of the street. On the right side of the street are the graceful rooflines of the **former French Legation** ❺. Turn left at the second alleyway, Taijichang Santiao, about 200m/yds beyond the Peking Club. French theologian Teilhard de Chardin, who lived in China from 1932 to 1946, founded an institute of geobiology on this street. Much of this area has been replaced with typical Chinese apartment blocks, but about 100m/yds along on the left, you can peer through the gates of the **former French Barracks**. The Soviet-style building in the centre is now the Chinese Workers' Union offices.

St Michael's Church

Continue for another 100m/yds along Taijichang Santiao and turn right. After another 100m/yds, you come to Dongjiaomin Xiang (Legation Street). Turn right again. Just before the next junction, about 200m/yds along on the right, is **St Michael's Church** ❻, an intimate little neo-Gothic church built by the French Vincentian Order in 1902. St Michael's was closed after the 1949 revolution, but was renovated and reopened in 1989. Services are held daily, and the staff and congregants are happy to let you stroll through to visit or pray. The figures of the saints above the chapel doors date all the way back to 1889 and some of the stained glass and ceramic tiles are original too.

Former Belgian Legation

Opposite the church, you can see the jagged brick rooflines and green tops of the **former Belgian Legation** ❼. Before 1900, this was the home of a high-level Chinese official, Xu Tong, who hated foreigners so much that he purportedly wished to cover his sedan

Above from far left: wrought-iron gate of the former Italian Legation; one of a pair of stone lions that guard the former French Legation; St Michael's Church; the leafy Foreign Legation Quarter makes for a nice walk.

French Road The mouth of Taijichang Toutiao is the site of Beijing's last remaining street sign in a foreign language: rue Hart.

Below: the former French Post Office is now home to a Sichuan restaurant

Decampment
Diplomats were living in the legation quarter right up until 1949, when they were asked to leave and the land was reclaimed by the government.

chair with their skin. He did his best to avoid them, but when the European Allied Armies entered Beijing in 1900 in reaction to the Boxer Rebellion, Xu Tong could take it no longer. He committed suicide.

From St Michael's Church, cross Taijichang Dajie and continue along Dongjiaomin Xiang. About 50m/yds past the junction, where two massive stone lions and two armed soldiers stand guard, are the red gates of another building belonging to the former French Legation. This is the former occasional residence of Cambodian King Norodom Sihanouk, a favour from the Chinese government when he went into exile. Next door is the home of Premier Wen Jiabao.

Across the road are the **former offices of Jardine Matheson**, one of the earliest Western trading companies in Asia. About 200m/yds further along on Dongjiaomin Xiang on the right, a tiny building with fancy brickwork, a zigzag roofline and arched windows now houses the authentically spicy Sichuan

restaurant Jingyuan Chuancai (tel: 6524 4156; daily 10.30am–2pm, 6.30–9.30pm). This was originally the **French Post Office ❽** and also the site of the original Beijing Hotel before it moved to its current location in 1900.

Former Spanish Legation
Next to the French Post Office is the **former Spanish Legation ❾**, where the protocol on the Boxer Rebellion was signed in 1901. The Spanish sold the corner lot to the Yokohama Specie Bank. Currently, the building houses Minsheng Bank. Empress Dowager Cixi was said to have borrowed money here just before the last dynasty fell. The valuables she put up as collateral were never reclaimed and are now in a collection in London. The bank stands on the corner of Dongjiaomin Xiang and Zhengyi Lu, the divided north–south street. 'Zhengyi' means 'justice', but the road used to be called Canal Street when it served as the Forbidden City's sewage outflow *(see p.34)*. It was filled in in 1925 to create the promenade between the two lanes.

Former Russian Legation
Cross Zhengyi Lu and continue on Dongjiaomin Xiang. On the right was once the site of the Russian Orthodox Mission, and was later the **Russian Legation ❿** and then the Soviet Legation. Russian Orthodox priests were some of the first foreigners to move into the area, well before it became a recognised neighbourhood for foreign representatives. Until 1991, there was a simple stone building here, probably the

Food and Drink

① **MAISON BOULUD**
Chi'enmen 23, 23 Qianmen Dongdajie; tel: 6559 9200; Mon–Fri 11.30am–2pm, Sat–Sun 11am–4pm, daily 6–10pm; $$$
Celebrity chef Daniel Boulud's innovative creations make this Beijing's finest French restaurant, famous for its service and impressive brunch menu (served weekends 11am–4pm).

② **RISTORANTE SADLER**
Chi'enmen 23, 23 Qianmen Dongdajie; tel: 6559 1399; daily 11.30am–2pm, 6–10.30pm; $$$
Fine Italian dining from the kitchen of Michelin-starred chef Claudio Sadler, with dishes paired to wines from an extensive list. The set lunch represents good value.

former Russian church. The expanded Supreme Court now stands here.

Opposite it is the **Police Museum** (Jingcha Bowuguan; Tue–Sun 9am–4pm; charge), showcasing the history of China's police force, forensic methods and an impressively comprehensive collection of old-fashioned torture devices. About 300m/yds further down on the left side of the street is a brick structure with a green roof. The **former Dutch Legation**, it is now the office of the Mao Zedong Mausoleum Administration. On the right is the former American legation compound, now a luxurious but troubled modern development, Chi'enmen 23 (tel: 6522 4848; daily 9am–6pm). This ambitious 'lifestyle development' has struggled to retain lesees but can still boast the highly regarded French restaurant **Maison Boulud**, see ⑪①, **Ristorante Sadler's** fine Italian fare, see ⑪②, as well as a large art exhibition space.

Backtrack on Dongjiaomin Xiang and make a left turn onto Zhengyi Lu for the final stretch. The area on the right side of Zhengyi Lu, north of Minsheng Bank, was the **former Japanese Legation** where the Chinese were forced to accept the infamous 'Twenty-One Demands' on 7 May 1915, whereby the Japanese obtained special rights over Manchuria. It now houses the Beijing mayor's office and the offices of the city government.

Former British Legation

The last, and possibly grandest relic on this walk is further along Zhengyi Lu on the left: the **former British Lega-**

tion ⑪. The British moved in after the Second Opium War of 1860 and expanded the area to create the largest territory held by foreigners. They retained this compound until 1959, but it is now occupied by the Ministries of State and Public Security – the Chinese version of the KGB. The grand gateway of the legation had housed a tiny shop for 10 years or so, and its enormous coat of arms was moved to London. The building has now been refitted with grand doors and put back into service.

Despite all the off-limits government buildings, the Legation Quarter is, at the time of writing, on the verge of being turned into a hot new neighbourhood – possibly once again home to rich and powerful foreigners. The old US embassy is scheduled to become home to a branch of Italy's Enoteca Pinchiorri, as well as several other projects of world-class chefs. Existing restaurants, such as Ice House and RBL, will move in too.

The Legation loop brings you to the northern end of Zhengyi Lu and onto Dongchang'an Jie, across from the Beijing Hotel.

Above from far left: gate motif of the former Belgian Legation; standing guard outside the Belgian Legation; the former Spanish Legation; the stoic former Dutch Legation.

Above: Beijing Hotel.

Below: the brick and stone facade of the former Spanish Legation.

3

LAMA TEMPLE, CONFUCIUS TEMPLE AND DITAN PARK

A tour of two temples with different philosophical traditions – Lamaist Buddhism and Confucianism. Round out with dinner and then dancing in Ditan Park, a favourite recreational playground of Beijing residents.

DISTANCE 1km (½ mile)
TIME Half a day, beginning from early afternoon till evening
START Lama Temple
END Peony Garden
POINTS TO NOTE
Take the subway to the Yonghegong stop. The sights are all within a 1km (½-mile) radius, so this is an easy walk.

Buddhism arrived in China from India in the 1st century, but Lamaism, the sect of Tibetan Buddhism that incorporates shamanist beliefs and practices, gained influence only after the Mongolians conquered Tibet and China in the 13th century. The Mongolian rulers had close relationships with Tibetan Buddhist leaders, and this led to the spread of Lamaism throughout China. During the Qing dynasty, Lamaism's influence was revived by the Manchus, who also practised the faith.

Golden Roof
The golden roof tiles of the Lama Temple are a remnant of its days as an imperial residence. Such tiles could only be used for imperial buildings and temples, or temples given a special imperial dispensation.

LAMA TEMPLE

Dating from 1694 and originally the private residence of Prince Yong, the fourth son of Emperor Kangxi, the **Lama Temple ❶** (Yonghegong; daily 9am–4pm; charge) was turned into a monastery after its owner became Emperor Yongzheng in 1723. According to custom, the former residence of a Son of Heaven had to be dedicated to religious purposes once he left. Hence in 1744, Yongzheng's son, Emperor Qianlong, established it as a monastery, and it soon flourished as a centre of Lamaist religion and art – one of the most notable outside of Tibet. At the same time, it offered the Qing rulers welcome opportunities for influencing and controlling their Tibetan and Mongolian subjects.

The temple, the most elaborately restored sacred building in Beijing, belongs to the Yellow Hat sect, though many traditional characteristics of that sect are missing. The monks do not wear yellow hats, for instance, or even the red robes common to Tibetan Buddhist lamas.

The Chinese government officially remains atheist, but with the reforms since 1978, churches and temples have been restored, along with the right to worship. These days, the surrounding neighbourhood caters to the Buddhist faithful – statuary and religious items are sold in shops along Yonghegong Dajie, and the smell of incense wafts through the streets.

Pavilion of 10,000 Happinesses

Today, about 70 monks live in the Lama Temple. Its five halls and three gates are laid out along a north-south axis. In each successive hall, the central Buddha is more imposing than the last.

Walk through the gardens before entering the inner courtyard, with its Bell and Drum towers and two pavilions. In the **Hall of Eternal Harmony** (Yonghegong) are three statues of the Buddha surrounded by 18 disciples. To the sides are buildings housing valuable *thangka* paintings and a mandala. In the three-storeyed section of the fifth hall, the **Pavilion of Ten Thousand Happinesses** (Wanfuge), is a 23m (75ft) high statue of the Buddha carved from a single piece of sandalwood. It took three years to transport the piece of sandalwood used for the statue from Nepal to Beijing; the building that houses the statue was built after it was completed.

Lamaism's roots lie in the mysterious rituals of the ancient Tibetan Bön religion. Look closely at the carvings and Tibetan *thangkas* in the side halls. One image shows the goddess Lamo riding a horse cloaked in the skin of her own son, who was sacrificed to show her detachment from the world.

CONFUCIUS TEMPLE

Your next stop is the **Confucius Temple ❷** (Kong Miao; daily 9am–4.30pm; charge), a tranquil former centre of scholarship. Go west on Guozijian Jie, the street opposite the Lama Temple across Yonghegong Dajie. The entrance to the Confucius Temple is 200m/yds on the right.

In the Confucius Temple's glorious

Above from far left: worshippers at the Lama Temple; offerings of incense; stone carving at the Pavilion of Ten Thousand Happinesses; prayer beads for sale.

Above: entrance to the Confucius Temple; drum and stele at the temple

Magic Well
The dry well in the courtyard was once said to bestow boundless literary talent upon any scholar who drank from it.

Gui Jie, Food Street
Just south of the Lama Temple is the western end of Gui Jie (also known as Ghost Street), an all-night dining boulevard illuminated by red lanterns and neon. This rowdy food street runs for over a kilometre and must be seen. If you can't get a table at Huajia Yiyuan, there are 200 other restaurants to choose from.

past, emperors came to offer sacrifices to Confucius at the **Hall of Great Achievement**, hoping for guidance in governance. Confucius was a teacher in the state of Lu (in present-day Shandong province) in the 6th century BC, about the same time the Buddha was teaching in India. The brand of Confucianism adopted by the emperors stressed order and so Confucianism was an important tool for keeping order across the vast and diverse nation.

Built in 1306 during the Yuan dynasty, this is the second-largest Confucian temple in China, after the one in Qufu, Confucius' hometown. The temple courtyard is filled with ancient pines, most of them several hundred years old. Combined with the ancient structures, they give one a sense of visiting the past. The temple's

prized possession is a collection of 190 steles inscribed with records of ancient civil service examinations.

IMPERIAL ACADEMY

Leave the temple, turn right and walk 200m/yds along Guozijian Jie for a brief look at the former **Imperial Academy** ❸ (Guozijian; daily 8.30am–5pm; charge), now the Capital Library. Once the highest educational institution in the land, it was where thousands of students and scholars came to listen to emperors expound Confucian classics. A set of steles commissioned by the Qing emperor Qianlong records 13 Confucian classics. Its 800,000 characters were engraved by a scholar over 12 years.

If you are interested in traditional Chinese handicrafts, browse the row of small shops at the far end of the Imperial Academy or along Guozijian Jie.

For refreshments, the burgeoning Wudaoying Hutong just west of the Lama Temple offers a number of bars and cafés including the reliable **Vineyard Café**, see ⑪①. A Buddhist-style vegetarian meal can be had at the popular **Xuxiangzhai Vegetarian Restaurant**, see ⑪②, across the street from the Confucius Temple. If it's already dinnertime consider making a worthwhile trip south to night-time food street Gui Jie, courtyard restaurant **Huajia Yiyuan** ⑪④ is always a reliable option

The landmark **Jin Ding Xuan**, see ⑪③, next to the entrance of Ditan Park, serves tasty dim sum at very reasonable prices 24-hours a day.

Confucianism Revival

Interestingly enough, Confucianism is regaining currency among some government leaders and intellectual circles. Following the quiet shelving of Communism and the amoral influences of commercial development, thinkers and theorists are groping for new ideas to help guide the country. Or, in this case, old ideas.

DITAN PARK

After dinner, proceed to **Ditan Park** ❹ (Ditan Gongyuan; daily 6am–9pm; charge). From Yonghegong Jie, walk north under Erhuan Lu (Second Ring Road). The south entrance is 300m/ yds north of the Yonghegong subway station. **Ditan** (Altar of the Earth; daily 8am–5pm; charge) was first built in 1530 and had a similar ritual function as the Temple of Heaven. Each year, on the summer solstice during the Ming and Qing dynasties, the emperor came here to make sacrifices to the Earth God. The altar, a round platform surrounded by two concentric square walls where the sacrifices were offered, was restored in the 1980s. Beijing residents come to Ditan Park in the early morning to dance and exercise.

PEONY GARDEN

After exploring the park, join in one of the most popular pastimes of modern China – ballroom dancing. Dance parties are held daily (May–Oct 6.30– 11am and 7–10pm, Nov–May 6.30– 11am; charge) in **Peony Garden** ❺ (Mudan Yuan), 200m/yds north of the altar. The park officially closes at 9pm but the gate is open all night to accommodate dancers. The park also holds one of Beijing's best Spring Festival temple fairs, with performances including Peking opera, folk dancing and re-enactments of Qing-dynasty imperial rituals, as well as stalls selling traditional snacks.

Food and Drink

① VINEYARD CAFÉ
31 Wudaoying Hutong; tel: 6402-7961; 11.30am–11.30pm; $
A well-known local eatery which is famed for its salads, frothy cappuccinos and decent wine list. The cafe gets particularly busy at the weekend.

② XUXIANGZHAI VEGETARIAN RESTAURANT
26 Guozijian Dajie; tel: 6404-6568; daily 11.30am–2pm and 5.30–9pm; $$
There is a grand tradition in Beijing of Buddhist vegetarian restaurants, many of which serve 'mock meat' – sausage, duck, fish and chicken – which is made with tofu and other vegetable products, and are surprisingly convincing. Xuxiangzhai gets extra credibility for its proximity to the Lama Temple, but really, it is the all-you-can-eat lunch buffets that make it popular.

③ JIN DING XUAN
South gate of Ditan Park; tel: 6429 6888; daily 24 hours; $$
It is almost enough just to look at Jing Din Xuan from a distance: the vast, three-storey restaurant features giant red lanterns and swooping blue roofs. A *renao* (boisterous) atmosphere is guaranteed inside and the wide range of dim sum is satisfying and inexpensive, if not the most authentic in town.

④ HUAJIA YIYUAN
235 Dongzhimennei Dajie (Gui Jie); tel: 6405 1908; 10.30am–4am; $$
An impressive traditional courtyard restaurant with a comprehensive picture menu which details a good amount of home-style dishes. Iy is a good idea to book ahead, if possible, to avoid dissapointment.

Above from far left: stele collection at the Confucius Temple; ornately carved incense urn at the Imperial Academy; kids in Ditan Park; Biyong Hall at the Imperial Academy.

Above: Ditan Park is a favourite with exercise enthusiasts, wedding couples and strollers.

THE LAKE DISTRICT

Once the pleasure ground of royalty, the Lake District now draws strollers and swimmers, as well as drinkers to its hip bars and cafés. Begin with a visit to the Drum and Bell towers, then snake your way around picturesque lakes to the imperial gardens of Beihai Park and Jade Island.

> **DISTANCE** 4km (2½ miles)
> **TIME** Half a day. This tour is designed for the afternoon, but can easily be adapted for the morning.
> **START** Drum and Bell towers
> **END** Beihai Park
> **POINTS TO NOTE**
> Take a taxi to the Drum and Bell towers, or walk south from the Gulou subway stop. This whole area is very pleasant to walk through; cycling is also an excellent option.

Beijing Snacks
You can find lots of Beijing's signature snacks in the alleyways around the Drum and Bell towers: *shaobing* (griddle-fried cakes with sesame seeds), *zha qiehe* (fried stuffed aubergine), *chao tianluo* (fried river snails), *jianbing* (crepes) and *douzhi* (milky dough made from beans).

The Lake District comprises Beihai Park, the former lakeside pleasure ground of the imperial family, and the Shichahai area, where a few other smaller 'back lakes' used to be the locale of many courtyard residences of Manchu princes and officials.

BELL AND DRUM TOWERS

Begin your tour at the grey **Bell Tower ❶** (Zhonglou) and the red **Drum Tower ❷** (Gulou; both daily 9am–4.30pm; charge). Kublai Khan had the original towers built nearby to serve as the imperial clock. The Drum Tower held 24 giant drums, which were beaten to mark the closing of the city gates and the passing of the night watches. The bell in the Bell Tower was struck to announce the time of day.

The towers were replaced in 1420 during the Ming dynasty. The Bell Tower, which was made of wood, was burned down and then rebuilt of stone in 1747. Structurally, the 33m (108ft) high Bell Tower is more interesting. Its stone staircase leads through a dark passageway reminiscent of medieval castles. In 1990, the bell was reinstalled in the tower. Since then the mayor has climbed the tower every Spring Festival to ring in the Lunar New Year. A chief attraction of the Drum Tower is the view from the top of the surrounding area of traditional courtyard houses. In the hall at the top is an original drum, damaged during the Opium Wars, and a full set of replicas, which can be beaten by curious sightseers. The courtyard between the two towers

Food and Drink 🍴

① BED

17 Zhangwang Hutong; tel: 8400 1554; daily 3pm–1am; $$
Bed's discerning clientele lounge on Chinese-style beds sipping mojitos or retire to the outside courtyard to ease the summer heat.

is perfect for lingering on a summer afternoon. Many pedicab tours also leave from here.

SURROUNDING HUTONG

Though this authentic and unrestored part of old Beijing constantly faces the threat of being bulldozed in the name of progress, it is, for now, a great place to explore. Zhangwang Hutong's history dates back to the Yuan dynasty and boasts two famous former residences: that of Reginald Johnston, the man who taught English to Emperor Puyi, and Princess Temple, once owned by an eunuch who served Empress Cixi. It also lays claim to **Bed**, see ⑪①, the city's hippest *hutong* bar, head-and-shoulders above Qianhai's neon-lit dives. Leading to Nanluogu Xiang *(see*

p.44) is Mao'er Hutong, one of the best-preserved *hutong* in Beijing. Its most famous distinguished resident was Wan Rong, last empress of China, who lived at No. 37 before marrying into the royal family. You can sneak into the central courtyard down a path to see the original supporting pillars and eaves.

HOUHAI

Start your walk around the Shichahai lakes, comprising Houhai, Xihai and Qianhai. The Shichahai lake system is man-made; during the Yuan dynasty it connected with reservoirs further north to supply the capital with water.

From the Drum and Bell towers, head south on Di'anmen Dajie and turn right into the first alleyway you come to, about 50m/yds along. This

Above from far left: swimming in Houhai in autumn; the bell in the Bell Tower; inside the Drum Tower; pedicab tour around the Lake District.

Bars Galore
The Lake District is peppered with tiny bars and restaurants.

Above from left: taking it easy by Xihai; view of Qianhai; Round City; Silver Ingot Bridge

Nanluogu Xiang
A detour worth making is Nanluogu Xiang – just follow Mao'er Hutong east from Di'anmen Dajie. It's one of the best shopping streets in town for quirky Chinese contemporary and retro gifts and clothes. Many of its shops are barely bigger than a large cupboard. There are also varied styles of cafes, bars and restaurants including neighbourhood mainstay Passby Bar, see ⑪⑦.

is **Yandai Xiejie**, which has become a major part of the **Houhai ❸** (Rear Lake) scene, packed with tiny café-bars and knick-knack shops. Another 150m/yds along is a junction where you should make a left turn. Ahead is a stone bridge called **Silver Ingot Bridge** (Yinding Qiao), which divides Houhai from Qianhai (Front Lake; *see p.45*). The two are part of a string of six lakes extending all the way from the north to the south of the old Inner City.

This area of town was home to princes and wealthy, powerful families during the Qing dynasty, hence the larger-than-average courtyard homes. During the early years of the PRC, the spacious homes were divided up among many families, as happened all over the city. The neighbourhood was then mostly ignored until the SARS epidemic in 2003. Convinced that the secluded area was somehow safer as the restaurants and bars are outdoors, people began flocking here, leading to the

establishment of a new bar area and the explosive growth that charac-terises the area today. Once again, wealthy people are buying the old courtyard homes and remodelling them, slowly restoring the neigh-bourhood to its historical character (albeit with the addition of neon).

If it is a nice day and you would like to stay by the lake, consider heading north from Silver Ingot Bridge. On the east edge of Houhai is the **Guanghua Buddhist Temple** (Guanghua Si; daily 8am–4pm; charge). Constructed during the Yuan dynasty, it is now home to the Beijing Buddhist Society. Relatively modest in size, it is well preserved and stocked with the usual colourful array of Bud-dhist statues and artefacts.

On the north-eastern edge of Houhai is the **former residence of Song Qin-gling** (Song Qingling Guju; daily 9am–4pm; charge), the wife of Sun Yat-sen. Song Qingling moved into the house in 1963 and lived there until her death in 1981. The guest room contains an exhi-bition of photographs, documents and objects from her life: her pampered Shanghai childhood as a daughter of one of China's most prominent families; her year as a student, her marriage to Sun Yat-sen, and her political activi-ties and support for the resistance to Japanese occupation.

Worth seeking out is **Jiumen Xiaochi**, see ⑪②, a collection of tra-ditional Beijing snack stalls re-created in a large courtyard which has a doorway guarded by white stone lions and large red lanterns.

Right: a statue in Pu An Hall.

XIHAI

Heading further north brings you to **Xihai** (West Lake), the only one of the lakes to have escaped gentrification. The willows hang lazily over the water, shading old fishermen, and locals stroll by the lake with their children – it is quite idyllic. Continuing to circle around the lakes, pass through Houhai Park, with the quietest boat-rental spot and well-known restaurant **Kong Yiji**, see ③, offering a very pleasant rooftop dining area. Branching off down Liuyin Hutong is **Gong Wang Fu** (Palace of Prince Gong), the world's largest extant courtyard house and a popular destination for tour groups. Prince Gong, the brother of Emperor Xian Feng, founded the Qing dynasty's department of foreign relations in 1861. His home and its 5.7-hectare (14-acre) grounds, including lush gardens, are now occupied by the China Conservatory of Music. The historic structures in the complex include Beijing's only preserved Qing-dynasty theatre.

QIANHAI

The most commercially developed part of Shichahai, **Qianhai** ❺ (Front Lake) is lined with bars, cafés and restaurants to draw in the passing crowds. Here, you will also encounter pedicabs offering *hutong* tours of the alleyways and sites around the lake. Expect to pay 180 yuan for 2½ hours, though reports of overcharging are common. Simply getting lost in the alleyways on foot by striking out westwards is a great way to see the neighbourhood; alternatively, rent a bicycle from one of the many rental outlets around the lake. **Lotus Lane** (Hehua Shichang), at the south-western corner of Qianhai, has cafés and restaurants like **South Silk Road**, see ④, and **Han Cang**, see ⑤, as well as some shops and high-end bars. There is nightly dancing and a variety of daytime activities,

Food and Drink

② JIUMEN XIAOCHI
1 Xiaoyou Hutong, Houhai; tel: 6402 5858; daily 10am–10pm; $
Beijing's most famous traditional snacks are offered under this roof. Enjoy boiled tripe, soft beancurd, rice cakes, wontons and more.

③ KONG YIJI
Shichahai Houhai Nanan; tel: 6618 4917; daily 10am–2pm and 4–10.30pm; $$
This popular themed diner re-creates the ancient flavours of Shaoxing, the southern hometown of famed writer Lu Xun. It is advisable to make a reservation.

④ SOUTH SILK ROAD
Lotus Lane; tel: 6615 5515; daily noon–midnight; $$
This specialises in Yunnanese food given a fusion twist. Don't expect large portions or low prices, but the food is exquisitely prepared and the atmosphere very classy. Sit on the walkway outside the restaurant, a better spot to see and be seen.

⑤ HAN CANG
Opposite Lotus Lane; tel: 6404 2259; daily 11am–3.30pm and 5–10.30pm; $$
Most people haven't heard of the Hakka people of Fujian, but one taste of their food and you are not likely to forget them. The chefs at Han Cang have developed a Hakka menu of great variety, but the dishes still stay close to their humble roots as simple mountain food. Try a wooden bucket of shrimp baked in salt, the river fish cooked in foil, and eggplant covered in fried garlic. All in a rough-hewn but classy atmosphere that makes for a perfect lakeside night.

Above: White
Dagoba on
Jade Island.

such as music and massages, around
the arched entrance to the lane.

BEIHAI PARK

Cross Di'anmen Xidajie to the north
entrance to **Beihai Park ⑥** (Beihai
Gongyuan or North Lake Park; daily,
summer 6.30am–10pm, winter 6am–
8pm; charge). The area around the
lake served as the imperial residence
for every dynasty that had its capital
in Beijing. After the end of the imperial era in 1925, Beihai Park was
opened to the public, though **Zhongnanhai** (Central and Southern Lake),
surrounded by a thick wall, remains
the cloistered domain of the Chinese
leadership as the site of the Politburo
and State Council offices (closed to
the public).

Beihai Park is great for strolls and
for going out on the lake in a rented
rowboat. On your boat cruise, first
skirt the western shore to see the
Nine Dragon Screen (Jiulongbi),
one of three in the city, and said to
offer protection from fire.

Miniature Western Heaven

About 200m/yds along the shore is
Miniature Western Heaven ⑦
(Xiaoxitian), built in 1770. A shrine
to Guanyin, the Goddess of Mercy, it
is a large square pagoda surrounded
by a moat and four guard towers.
Then, backtrack to the **Five Dragon
Pavilion** (Wulongting), which is
named after the zigzagging walkways
linking them.

Jade Island

Just north of the Five Dragon
Pavilion, board a ferry to **Jade Island
⑧** (Qiong Dao; every half hour, daily
9am–6pm). The boat stops in front of
Fangshan Restaurant, see ⑪⑥, in
the **Hall of Ripples** (Yilantang)
complex. This is a potential dinner
(or lunch) destination, but explore
the lovely imperial gardens first.

Turn right onto the covered
walkway that leads to the **Pavilion of
Shared Coolness** (Xiexiuting) and
take the stone path up the hill. Climb
to the **Plate for Gathering Dew**
(Chenglupan), a bronze figure of a

Right: Nine Dragon
Screen.

man holding a container over his head. Emperor Qianlong built this whimsical tribute to a Han-dynasty emperor who believed the dew was an elixir for immortality. On the north-west side of the hill is the **Building for Reading Old Inscriptions** (Yuegulou), which has stone tablets covered with 6th- and 7th-century calligraphy. On the summit is the **White Dagoba ❾** (Baita), a 35m (115ft) shrine dating from 1651, built by Shunzhi, the first Qing-dynasty emperor to reign in Beijing, to commemorate the first visit to Beijing by a Dalai Lama.

Descend on the south side of the hill. Pass through the **Hall of Universal Peace** (Pu'andian), an official meeting room in the Qing dynasty. The last stop is the Lamaist **Temple of Eternal Peace** (Yong'ansi). When you emerge on the south side of the island, you come to an elegant marble bridge connecting the island to the shore. From here, you can see, or cross the bridge to visit, the **Round Town** (Tuancheng; daily 8am–4.30pm; charge). It was the administrative centre of 15th-century Dadu during the Yuan dynasty.

Leave Beihai Park by the south gate, where taxis await.

Above from far left: tea house in Behai Park; boating on Behai; a woman exercising in Behai Park; Round City.

Food and Drink 🍴

⑥ **FANGSHAN RESTAURANT**
Inside the east gate of Beihai Park; tel: 8401 1889; daily 11am–2pm and 5–8pm; $$$
You'll be fed like an emperor in sumptuous rooms once inhabited by princes, with dishes often unrecognisable. The food can be more exciting to look at than to eat, and consists largely of delicacies more impressive for their rarity than their flavour. All the same, a meal here is an experience you won't repeat anywhere else.

⑦ **PASSBY BAR**
108 Nanluogu Xiang; tel: 8403 8004; daily 9.30am–2am; $$
The first bar on Nanluoguxiang is still popular for its outside courtyard, library of travel books and western food.

Cycling

Bicycles can be hired from a point just east of the Drum Tower or at various spots around Houhai for about 10 yuan per hour, plus a deposit. For the more serious rider, Natooke (19 Wudaoying Hutong; tel 8402 6925; daily 10.30am–7pm) hires vintage Flying Pigeon and fixed gear bikes by the day. Apart from the pedestrianised Lotus Lane, all roads and alleyways around the Lake District can be navigated by bike. Latching on to one of the mini cavalcades of pedicabs that traverse the area will get you a free tour of the major historic spots or simply head off on your own to explore the vernacular architecture of the hutong and their assorted workshops, chess rooms and snack stalls.

5

TEMPLE OF HEAVEN

Early-morning exercise rituals in the Temple of Heaven Park, followed by an exploration of the temple complex, a stop at the Natural History Museum and shopping at Hongqiao Market.

DISTANCE 3½km (2 miles)
TIME Half a day
START Temple of Heaven Park
END Hongqiao Market
POINTS TO NOTE

The Tiantandongmen subway stop makes a convenient arrival point for the entrance via the east gate and along the Long Corridor. Alternatively, take a taxi to the south gate and approach the iconic Hall of Prayer for Good Harvests as the emperor did.

Pathway to Heaven
Entering the park by the southern entrance you will approach the Hall of Prayer for Good Harvests via the Danbi Bridge, the route the emperor would take to 'step up to Heaven'.

The Temple of Heaven complex was originally constructed between 1406 and 1429 under Emperor Yongle of the Ming dynasty. Every year at the time of the winter solstice, the emperor would come here in a magnificent procession lasting several days to honour his ancestors and to pray for a good harvest in the season to come. There is an audio tour, available in most major languages, at the gates.

TEMPLE OF HEAVEN PARK

Enclosed by a 5km (3-mile) -long wall, the **Temple of Heaven Park ❶** (Tiantan Gongyuan; park daily 6am–9pm, temple daily 8am–5.30pm; separate charges for park and temple)

is the best place in Beijing to catch a glimpse of some traditional, and some not-so-traditional, forms of Chinese culture. Along the paths and among the trees, Beijing residents practise *qigong* to strengthen their internal systems through concentration and slow-motion exercises that stimulate breathing and circulation. Plan to arrive by 7am or earlier if you want to see early-morning enthusiasts of *qigong*, *taiji*, calligraphy, Peking opera and kite-flying. The **Long Corridor** (Changlang) on the east side of the Hall of Prayer for Good Harvests *(see below)* is the best spot for seeing activities of all kinds.

TEMPLE COMPLEX

The park is round in the north, representing Heaven, and square in the south, representing Earth. Walk through the park to get to the city's most elegant and most recognised structure, the **Hall of Prayer for Good Harvests** (Qiniandian).

Hall of Prayer for Good Harvests

This exquisite example of a Chinese wooden building was constructed without nails or cement. The round hall is 40m (130ft) high, its three levels covered with deep-blue tiles symbolising Heaven. The roof is supported by 28 pillars: the four central pillars represent the four seasons; the double ring of 12 pillars represents the 12 months and the traditional divisions of the Chinese day (each comprising two hours). Intricate carpentry created the dome high overhead; below are

thrones where tablets commemorating ancestors were placed. Destroyed several times, the hall was rebuilt in 1890.

Imperial Vault of Heaven

Head south to the **Imperial Vault of Heaven** (Huangqiongyu), which is much smaller but has similar deep-blue roof tiles representing Heaven. Ancestral tablets were stored here until they were needed for prayer ceremonies. The imperial vault is now best known for its acoustics. If you stand on the first of the **Three Echo Stones** (Sanyinshi) in front of the entrance and clap, you will hear a single echo. Do the same on the second stone, you will hear a double echo; and on the third, a triple echo. Whisper into the **Echo Wall** that encloses the courtyard around the hall, and another person will be able to hear every word anywhere along the wall. Walk south to the **Altar of Heaven** (Yuanqiu), where three concentric terraces stand inside two enclosures – one square (symbolising Earth) and one round (symbolising Heaven). Animal sacrifices took place inside the square enclosure while the emperor prayed at the centre of the mound.

Hall of Abstinence

On the way to the west exit of the temple, you pass through the courtyard of the **Hall of Abstinence** (Zhaigong). The hall has a double moat spanned by a series of fine stone bridges, and its courtyard has a beautiful drum and bell tower. Twice a year, the emperor would spend a night of fasting and celibacy in the hall prior to

Above from far left: Hall of Prayer for Good Harvests; Beijing residents partake in some traditional drumming and dancing in the Temple of Heaven Park; inside the Hall of Prayer for Good Harvests; Hall of Abstinence.

Above: Echo Wall; Imperial Vault of Heaven.

Homage to the Heavenly Emperor
The Hall of Prayer for Good Harvests contains a plaque dedicated to the Emperor of Heaven – this was the closest the earthly emperor and his heavenly counterpart ever came to one another.

Above from left:
Natural History
Museum; Hongqiao
Market; Wan Fung
Art Gallery; view of
the Forbidden City
moat in the evening.

the sacrificial rites the next morning. These rituals, which survived until 1914, go back 4,000 years.

NATURAL HISTORY MUSEUM

Leave by the west gate, just north of the Palace of Abstinence. Outside the gate, you come to the main north-south street, Tianqiao Nandajie, after about 100m/yds. Turn right and walk about 300m/yds to the **Natural History Museum ❷** (Ziran Bowuguan; daily 8.30am–5pm; charge). This is most famous for its large collection of dinosaur bones, gathered from other

parts of China and Mongolia, as well as the endless numbers of dinosaur models. The exhibits on humanity's descent from apes are mildly interesting, while the human specimens are downright eerie.

HONGQIAO MARKET

A five-minute taxi ride will take you to the north-eastern corner of the park where the **Hongqiao Market ❸** (Hongqiao Shichang; daily 8.30am–7pm), or Pearl Market, stands across the street. This indoor market has everything from meat and spices to toys, clothes and antiques but it is known as the best place in Beijing to buy pearls. Once there, be sure to head to the fifth floor for the best available view of the Temple of Heaven Park.

Backtrack 300m/yds towards the north gate of the Temple of Heaven Park to arrive at **Old Beijing Noodle**, see ⑪①, the ideal spot for lunch with a friendly local atmosphere and noodles served with a touch of performance.

Hongqiao Market

The best and the worst pearls can be found at Hongqiao Market. Be careful when making purchases – if you're not knowledgeable about pearls, consider bringing a friend who is, or doing some research ahead of time. Sellers will often scrape the surface of a pearl to show that it is not simply a painted bead. This is not a fail-safe sign of a real pearl, but it can help you avoid the more flagrant fakes. There are wild and cultivated pearls at an enormous range of prices, as well as other precious gems such as jade and amber, at Hongqiao Market.

Food and Drink 🍴

① OLD BEIJING NOODLE
29 Chongwenmen Dajie; tel: 6705 6705; daily 11am–2.30pm and 5–9pm; $
This restaurant has revived the lively tradition of old-style Beijing fast food with hand-pulled noodles and other affordable dishes served in a rowdy atmosphere. *Zhajiang Mian*, noodles, served up with soybean paste and vegetables, are Beijing's most famous.

TIANANMEN AND SANLITUN AT NIGHT

See a more tranquil side to the Tiananmen area, then trawl the buzzing Donghuamen Night Market, and onto Beijing's original bar street.

Night-time sees a very different side to the Tiananmen area. By day, the Forbidden City and Tiananmen Square are tourist magnets; by night the outer wall of the Forbidden City is hauntingly peaceful. One reason could be the unspoken sense of taboo or superstition that many Beijingers still feel around the former residence of the emperors. Nearly a hundred years after the end of the empire, the old injunction against commoners entering the palace has yet to fade completely in the minds of Beijingers, and many will not visit at night.

ART GALLERIES

Begin your tour at the **Imperial City Art Gallery** ❶ (Huangcheng Yishuguan; daily 10am–5.30pm), one of the city's newer museums, located in Changpuhe Park. The exhibits here are artefacts and artworks from the Forbidden City, including clothing and sumptuous articles of daily use. In addition, there is usually also a high-profile exhibition of art from abroad – Picasso figured in a show once.

Across Nanchizi Dajie from the Imperial City Art Gallery is **Huangshicheng** ❷, the oldest-surviving imperial archival vault in the country. Built in 1536, it held national records, imperial genealogies and legal compendia during the Ming and Qing dynasties. It now houses two galleries of interest: the **Wan Fung Art Gallery** (tel: 6523 3320; Mon 12pm–6pm, Tue–Sun 10am–6pm) and the **New Art Centre** (tel: 6528 9103; daily 9am–5.30pm). Both galleries specialise in contemporary, though not necessarily modern, art by local Chinese ink artists.

TIANANMEN SQUARE

After your tour of the galleries, leave Nanchizi Dajie and head to **Tiananmen Square** ❸ for the flag-lowering ceremony, which is held at sunset, around 5.30pm in winter and 7.30pm in summer. The ceremony is one of the last

Above: flag-lowering ceremony on Tiananmen Square.

Above from left: night-time Tiananmen Square; entering The Courtyard restaurant; the bright lights of Sanlitun bar district.

few Soviet-style rituals China still practises. To encourage patriotism, it was beefed up with more soldiers and a taller flagpole. Hundreds gather each evening to watch the military drill and the flag-lowering, and thousands come on 1 May (International Workers' Day) and 1 October (China's National Day), although it is hard to know what draws them precisely. But soon after the flag descends, quiet settles over the square. After the lights on the Monument to the People's Heroes and the Tiananmen Gate come on, the square seems a very different place. You might consider a slight detour for a quiet stroll around the National Centre for the Performing Arts to view its other-worldly form reflected on the surrounding moat.

Approaching the Forbidden City

Begin your walk by crossing under Dongchang'an Jie via the pedestrian tunnel. Walk through the Tiananmen Gate and follow the 600m/yd approach from the Tiananmen Gate to the Meridian Gate (Wumen), the entrance to the Forbidden City. When you reach the Meridian Gate, take a right and walk along the perimeter of the Forbidden City, between its high wall and the moat. With just a few bicycles whirring past and couples whispering on park benches, it is easy to imagine being transported back to a different century.

DONGHUAMEN

Leave the Forbidden City via the side gate and take an immediate left. This road runs between the palace and the moat, so you won't get lost. After 50m/yds, it turns right, goes straight for another 400m/yds and turns left where there is another 50m/yd stretch. At this point you see the east gate of the Forbidden City on the left. Located here as well is **The Courtyard**, see 🍴①, one of the top-rated restaurants in the city. The cigar lounge on its third floor is a great place for a pre-night-market drink. The road bends right and becomes **Donghuamen Night Market** ❹ (Donghuamen Yeshichang), where you can find some of the most varied snacks and street food in town. Try a bowl of red-bean porridge or grilled quail if you are feeling peckish, or a stick of fried locusts if you dare.

If you need a more substantial meal, you are in luck, as you have just reached a strip of restaurants largely owned by, and catering to, overseas Chinese. There is good seafood and Cantonese restaurants on both sides of the street, such as the swanky **Hong Kong Food City**, see 🍴②.

WANGFUJING STREET

After dinner, continue east to **Wangfujing Dajie** ❺, Beijing's premier shopping street *(see p.32)*. Head north up on Wangfujing Dajie to **St Joseph's Cathedral** ❻ (Dongtang) *(see p.33)*. Also known as the East Cathedral and illuminated at night, it was originally built in the 17th century. It has been restored many times and is now spruced up as the district's main feature.

SANLITUN

To round off the evening, hop into a taxi to **Sanlitun**, a perennial favourite on Beijing's nightlife scene. Its 'Bar Street' runs along Sanlitun Lu, north of

the Workers' Stadium, though the aggressive touts here mostly succeed only in pulling in tourists. Those in the know head straight to Nali Patio – a white, Mediterranean-style plaza packed with reasonable restaurants and bars – or to Sanlitun Houjie, behind the 3.3 Mall and parallel to Sanlitun Lu. Sanlitun Houjie, a rather grubby street that is slowly going upmarket, has two decent pubs: The Tree *(see p.119)* and First Floor *(see p.118)*. There are some nice outdoor and rooftop spots north of Sanlitun Lu and along The Workers' Stadium on West Street. At Chaoyang Park's east gate is a bar district patronised mainly by foreign business people.

Bar Life

Nightspots have mushroomed in several areas in Beijing in recent years. Besides Sanlitun and Wudaokou, there is Women's Street in the Chaoyang embassy district, with similar bar and restaurant offerings as Sanlitun. The area north of the Workers' Stadium offers another rash of nightspots (above). The Lake District around Houhai and Lotus Lane has quieter, although still vibrant, alternatives.

Food and Drink 🍴

① THE COURTYARD
95 Donghuamen Lu; tel: 6526 8883; www.courtyardbeijing.com; daily 6–10pm; $$$
Once rated one of the top 50 restaurants in the world by *Condé Nast Traveller* magazine, The Courtyard definitely has an atmosphere to match its reputation. Gaze out over the Forbidden City moat as you dine on French and European food, or make a selection from the very extensive wine cellar.

② HONG KONG FOOD CITY
18 Dong'anmen Dajie; tel: 6525 7349; daily 11am–midnight; $$
One of Beijing's few options for authentic Cantonese dim sum. *Chashao bao* (steamed pork buns) and roast goose are the favourites. The atmosphere may be fancy, but this place is still suited for the kind of meals that dim sum is made for – long afternoons with family and friends, with round after round of tasty snacks.

Opposite: street food at Donghuamen Night Market.

7

DAZHALAN AND LIULICHANG

Walk through the old neighbourhood of Dazhalan with its warren of shops, into Liulichang, a restored section of the old city that is jam-packed with old shops selling curios and antiques, then onto the famous Ox Street Mosque.

DISTANCE 5km (3 miles)
TIME Half a day
START Qianmen
END Ox Street Mosque
POINTS TO NOTE

Exploring the dirty, unreconstructed **hutong** of the Qianmen area is half the fun of a visit. Some common sense is needed in judging the standard of hygiene of the food on offer, however.

Above: an alleyway in Southern Beijing; a popular mode of transport.

The southern area of Beijing has long been the poorer side of town, ever since the Manchu invasion of 1644 relocated the local Han Chinese here – away from the nobles and military officials who chose to reside in ele-

gant homes further north. The streets deviate from the strict grid pattern of most of Beijing, the pavements are narrower and the drainage inferior. A massive development project centred on Qianmen Dajie in recent years has meant the beginning of the end for many of the old alleyways with their messy but characteristic way of life. The Muslim Quarter still offers a more organic and authentic experience within easy reach of the city centre.

QIANMEN AREA

Arriving at Qianmen subway station, use the southern exit to emerge at the entrance to **Qianmen Dajie ❶**, with the glamorous facade of **Capital M**, see ⑪①, and a slightly anachronous tourist tram to greet you. This pedestrianised shopping street is done up in traditional style and stretches into the distance with many smaller streets, often packed with tiny snack shops and food stalls, branching off east and west. High rents have driven many traditional businesses away from the Qianmen area since its makeover but the local government has been experimenting with subsidising the city's time-honoured brands operating here in hopes of keeping the 'old Beijing' theme alive.

Opened in 2011, the **Xianyukou Food Street** is mostly lined with traditional Beijing businesses. Enter through a gate marked by two giant red fish and sample wares such as stewed liver and red bean paste-filled rice cakes. There are also dumplings and steamed buns on sale for the less adventurous.

DAZHALAN STREET

Dazhalan Jie ❷, a bustling *hutong* heading west of Qianmen Dajie boasts a 600-year heritage and is famous for its old shops. The name Dazhalan (often refered to as 'Dashilar' in Beijing dialect) literally means 'big stockades', and is an echo of Ming times when the streets were closed off at the evening curfew.

Traditional Shops

About 20m/yds along on the right is a building with extravagant wrought-iron gatework in green. This is **Hou Cheng Yi** (daily 9am–8.30pm), with a wide choice of fabrics on the second floor.

Two doors down is **Ruifuxiang Silk and Cotton Fabric Store** (daily 9am–8pm), with a somewhat pretentious marble entrance. Ruifuxiang was built in 1893 by a Shandong businessman and catered to society's upper crust, including the wives and concubines of the imperial court.

At No. 22 Dazhalan Xijie is **Zhang Yiyuan Tea Shop** (daily 8am–8pm), with bas-relief floral designs under its windows. More than a century old,

Zhang Yiyuan stocks a diversity of Chinese tea leaves. Next door at No. 24 is **Tongrentang Traditional Medicine Shop** (daily 8am–7.30pm), once responsible for keeping secret medicinal recipes for emperors. It has been here since 1669, and its pharmacists still weigh age-old herbal remedies with hand-held scales.

A little further down, at No. 36, is the grand entrance to **Daguanlou** (daily 9am–midnight), the oldest operating cinema in the world. Originally a teahouse that put on opera performances, the venue started to show foreign short films between acts in 1903.

YANGMEI ALLEYWAY

About 300m/yds further along Dazhalan Jie, you arrive at another junction. Turn right and then, another 30m/yds on, turn left. This is **Yangmei Hutong ❸**, a typical alleyway with children and old people in the street and the smells of cooking and communal toilets mingled together. Most of the doors lead into *siheyuans*, courtyards with rooms on four sides facing inwards.

Above: Liulichang is an excellent place to stock up on souvenirs such as Chinese seals, Buddha images and Mao's Little Red Books.

Food and Drink 🍴

① **CAPITAL M**
2 Qianmen Dajie; tel: 6702 2727; daily 11.30am–10.30pm; $$$
The sister restaurant to Shanghai's famous M on the Bund. The Qianmen location affords impressive terrace views across Tiananmen Square to match the glamorous interior and fine continental dining. Afternoon tea served from 2–5pm.

Above from left:
Ruifuxiang Fabric
Store; window display
of traditional Chinese
shoes; curio shop in
Liulichang; Chinese
paint brushes.

Historic Theatre
Beijing's first
movie house, the
Daguanlou Cinema,
opened on Qianmen
Dajie in 1911.

Below: Neiliansheng
Shoe Store dates
back to the 1850s.

LIULICHANG STREET

After another 400m/yds, Yangmei
Hutong takes a little jog to the right.
There is an antiques shop on your left.
Turn left onto **Liulichang Jie ❹**,
packed with shops selling curios and
antiques. This has been a retail area for
books and antiques for over 300 years.

During the Ming dynasty, Liulichang, which means 'glazed-tile
factory', was one of the areas where
tiles were made for imperial buildings. Later, it developed into a
cultural centre for scholar-officials,
who came here to stock up on calligraphy materials, books and seals.

These days, Liulichang has reverted to
its old function as a purveyor of paper
and inks, patronised by serious callig-

raphers. Check out **Rongbaozhai** (daily
9am–5.30pm), a 17th-century shop at
No. 19 Liulichang Xijie. It is famous for
its range of watercolour paintings, calligraphy works, charcoal rubbings and
painting materials. **Daiyuexuan** (daily
9am–5.30pm) at No. 73 is the place to
go for quality paintbrushes, which it has
been selling since 1916.

ZHENGYICI PEKING OPERA THEATRE

Continue on to Nanxinhua Dajie and
turn right. A few hundred metres
north, before the Hepingmen subway
stop, turn right onto Xiheyan Dajie. In
the alleyway is the **Zhengyici Peking
Opera Theatre ❺** (Zhengyici Xilou;
performances every evening; tel: 8315
1649). More than 330 years old, it is
the only traditional theatre in the city
to have its original, all-wood construction completely preserved. There are
two storeys from which to view the
action, which takes place on a stage
that is open on three sides.

TEMPLE OF THE SOURCE OF BUDDHIST DOCTRINE

A subway journey from Hepingmen to
Caishikou subway station (change at
Xuanwumen) takes you to Guangan-
mennei Dajie. Head east for 200m/yds
then south along Xizhuan Hutong to
find **The Temple of the Source of Buddhist Doctrine ❻** (Fayuansi; Thur–Tue
8.30–11.30am and 1.30–3.30pm;
charge). The maze of *hutong* can be confusing so you might consider taking a

taxi here. This is one of the oldest-
surviving Buddhist temples in Beijing,
built in AD645, and houses the Buddhist Academy. The academy trains
novice monks, who are then despatched
to monasteries across China. It has a
library of more than 100,000 precious
texts and an exhibition of Buddhist
sculptures, some dating from the Han
dynasty. The complex has six halls, lying
beyond the main entrance Shanmen
(Mountain Gate). In the first temple
courtyard, two bronze lions guard the
Hall of the Celestial Kings (Tianwang-
dian). Enthroned in the middle of the
hall is a Milefo, a laughing, fat-bellied
Buddha. The Hall of Heroes (Daxiong-
baodian) contains a Buddha surrounded
by 18 Luohan, the lowest rank in the
Buddhist divine hierarchy. This is
reached by leaving the first hall and
crossing a garden with a bronze caul-
dron and stone steles. In the last hall is
a reclining Buddha and a Guanyin Bod-
hisattva with 1,000 arms. Stroll past the
gardens on Fayuansi Qianhutong
towards Niu Jie (Ox Street).

OX STREET MOSQUE

Built in AD996, **Ox Street Mosque** ❼
(Niujie Qingzhensi; daily 8am–4pm;

charge), has all the features of mosques
found elsewhere in the world – a
minaret, Arabic inscriptions and a
prayer hall facing Mecca – but all in
Chinese-style buildings. Islam arrived in
China during the Tang dynasty via Arab
merchants, and Muslims now live in all
parts of the country.

This mosque is a gathering place for
the city's Muslim community. Female
visitors need not cover up their heads
to enter, but shorts and short skirts are
not allowed (the caretaker can lend you
a pair of baggy pants). Non-Muslims
cannot enter the prayer hall. Right
behind the main entrance is a hexagonal
building, the Tower for Observing the
Moon (Wangyuelou). Every year, at the
beginning and at the end of the fasting
month of Ramadan, the imam climbs
the tower to observe the waxing and
waning of the moon and to determine
the exact length of the period of fasting.

Hui shops and schools in the area
around the mosque are signs of the
community's unique Muslim background. Round the day off with
dinner at **Da Shun Tang**, see 🍴②,
where you have the chance to try
some Muslim dishes.

8

THE SUMMER PALACE

A tour which takes you through the magnificent landscaped gardens and lavish palaces built outside Beijing for the pleasure of the Empress Dowager Cixi in 1888.

Mystic Waters
Kunming Lake was used to predict national trends in the Qing dynasty – stillness or turbulence indicated calm or storms in the future.

DISTANCE 2km (1½ miles)
TIME Half a day
START The north gate
END Sackler Gallery
POINTS TO NOTE

To get to the palace, take the subway to either Xiyuan or Beigongmen stations, or you can take a taxi. Though the basic layout can be traversed in half a day, the huge park can provide a much longer walk for those who want to see more of its sights.

The **Summer Palace** (Yiheyuan; daily, summer 6.30am–8.30pm, winter 7am–7pm; charge) was built in the late Qing dynasty to replace the nearby Old Summer Palace (Yuanmingyuan; *see opposite*), which was destroyed by the European Eight Allied Armies in 1860 in the Second Opium War. In 1900, a large part of the palace was destroyed by Europeans during the Boxer Rebellion, when the anti-foreign rebels, mainly practitioners of Chinese boxing, laid siege to foreigners in Beijing.

The notoriously erratic Empress Dowager Cixi fulfilled a wonderful but expensive dream in 1888 when she created this sprawling playground – the grounds cover more than 30 sq km (10 sq miles) – using 30 million taels of silver that was originally intended for a naval fleet. Cixi loved her new creation. She and her entourage effectively abandoned the Forbidden City and ruled China from here for 20 years until her death in 1908. The debate on Cixi's direct role in imperial China's decline continues, but the most widely accepted version of events begins with Cixi as a concubine of the third rank. She placed herself on the Dragon Throne after the death of Emperor Xianfeng in 1861, and ruled unscrupulously for the next 50 years in the name of her child.

Arriving at Beigongmen subway station leads you into the park via Suzhou Street, created as a replica of a 19th-century canal-side shopping area in Suzhou, for Cixi and her court to shop without mixing with ordinary mortals

Longevity Hill

Ascend from Suzhou Street into the square towers and stupas of the **Sumeru Temple** (Xumilingjing) and then down into the **Temple of the Sea of Wisdom ❶** (Zhihuihai) at the top of Longevity Hill. Built in 1750, the temple is covered with countless Buddhas in the niches of its greenish-yellow ceramic facade. Many of the lower Buddhas were either smashed or beheaded by Red Guards during the Cultural Revolution. There are good views of the lake from this spot and a wonderful panoramic view of the whole palace further on at the massive octagonal **Pagoda of Buddhist Virtue**

❷ (Foxiangge), the highest point of the park. Connected to the pagoda by decorated corridors is the **Hall of Virtuous Light** (Dehuidian) and the **Hall of Dispelling Clouds ❸** (Paiyundian), which comprises of 21 rooms housing some valuable artefacts, including the throne Cixi would sit upon to receive gifts on her birthday. Adjacent, on the west side, is one of the few buildings that survived the destruction of 1900 undamaged, the **Pavilion of Precious Clouds ❹** (Baoyunge). In Cixi's day, Lamaist monks gathered here to pray on the 1st and 15th day of every lunar month. Its stepped roof and its beams, columns and struts, make it look like a wooden, yet they were all cast from bronze in 1750.

Above: Marble Boat on Kunming Lake, where Empress Dowager Cixi once took tea; Hall of Benevolence and Longevity; musician performing at the Garden of Virtue and Harmony; temples of the Summer Palace.

Old Summer Palace

The Old Summer Palace (Yuanmingyuan) is equally worth visiting. This sprawling complex was once the playground of Qing emperors. Utterly unlike its newer neighbour, it was distinguished from other imperial palaces by its unique architecture. Designed and built by European architects, it blended a variety of European styles into a dreamlike jumble that placed formal labyrinths next to Roman-style villas. The Old Summer Palace took the brunt of the invasion of the European Eight Allied Armies in 1860, and in subsequent decades was further dismantled by local residents. It has been left more or less in its original state of destruction, outfitted with signage as a reprimand to forgetful Westerners.

Above from left:
souvenirs on Suzhou
Street; Long Corridor;
child's play in Beijing.

The Long Corridor

The **Long Corridor** ❺ (Changlang) is a magnificent example of a Chinese covered walkway. It runs parallel to the shore of Kunming Lake for 728 metres (798 yards). The ceilings and rafters are decorated with countless bird-and-flower motifs. At the end of the Long Corridor lies the famous **Marble Boat** ❻ (Qingyanfang), misleadingly named as it is not made of marble nor capable of floating. Cixi is thought to have squandered a fortune on this, money that should have gone to the Chinese navy. Make a stop at **Tingliguan** resturant, see ⑪①, which is close by.

Above: Bridge of
Seventeen Arches;
the Pagoda of
Buddhist Virtue
towers over the Hall
of Dispelling Clouds;
signage at the Hall of
Virtuous Light.

Boat Tour

From the Marble Boat, it is possible to cross **Kunming Lake** ❼ (Kunming Hu) by 'dragon boat', landing either on Nanhudao (Southern Lake Island) or on the neighbouring mainland just south of the Hall of Jade Ripples (Yulantang). Close to the bridge leading to Nanhudao crouches the **Bronze Ox** (tongniu). Its task is to pacify the water spirits and to protect the surrounding land from floods. **The Bridge of Seventeen Arches** ❽ (Shiqikongqiao) crosses the water in a supremely graceful curve, linking Nanhudao with the mainland. On the small island itself is the **Dragon**

King's Temple ❾ (Longwangmiao) where Cixi would pray for rain in times of drought.

The Eastern Shore

The **Hall of Jade Ripples** ❿ is a courtyard building that served as Emperor Guangxu's bed chamber during his visits, and his prison after Cixi supposedly put him under house arrest here for his recklessness at attempting to reform a crumbling dynasty by opening China to foreign ideas in 1898. Not far from the Hall of Jade Ripples, the refurbished **Hall of Laughter** ⓫ (Daxilou) was where Cixi and her court sat to view performances at an open-theatre called the Garden of Virtue and Harmony (Deheyuan). Today, Deheyuan serves as a theatre museum. The lavish **Hall of Benevolence and Longevity** ⓬ (Renshoudian), with its opulent furnishings and objets d'art, is where Cixi held audiences with ministers and handled other state business in the summer.

SACKLER GALLERY

If you have time on the way back to the city, visit the **Sackler Gallery** (daily 9am–4.30pm; charge) on Beijing University's beautiful campus. Enter by the west gate. The gallery is the second building on the left after the bridge. View artefacts spanning some 280,000 years, which for seven decades were stacked in the archaeology department. The display is well designed and the museum is not too large, so you can pass from Paleolithic humanoids to the Qing dynasty in 45 minutes.

Food and Drink 🍴

① TINGLIGUAN
Near the Marble Boat; tel: 6288 1955; www.tingliguan.com;
daily 11am–2pm and 5–7pm; $$$
Tingliguan serves dishes that were popular at the imperial court.
Fresh fish caught from Kunming Lake is a house speciality.

BEIJING FOR KIDS

Beijing's most famous attractions, such as the Forbidden City or the Great Wall, may not always appeal to younger travellers. But the city can also offer entertainment for children – and relief for their parents.

Beijing has both good and bad points when it comes to travelling with children. On the one hand, the city can appear drab and unexciting, and it seems like there is nowhere that is safe from swerving taxis. On the other hand, Beijingers are enormously protective towards children. You will find that the average stranger will go out of his or her way to keep your little ones from danger (though you may get a scolding afterwards). Moreover, the city does conceal a number of pleasant locations that, once discovered, are perfect for keeping your children entertained.

DISTANCE 3½km (2 miles)
TIME Half a day
START FunDazzle
END Ritan Park
POINTS TO NOTE
Take a taxi to the south gate of the Workers' Stadium. You can either take a taxi or walk from the Workers' Stadium to Ritan Park. The walk ends at the south gate of Ritan Park, within walking distance of the Yong'anli subway stop.

FUNDAZZLE

Parents in Beijing know that for kids of younger ages, **FunDazzle ❶** (Fandoule; east of the south gate of the Workers' Stadium; tel: 6506 9066; daily 9am–5.30pm; charge) provides endless entertainment, with arcade games, jungle gyms, ball rooms and more. Most younger kids are willing to stay all day.

BLUE ZOO

Not far to the west from FunDazzle is the **Blue Zoo ❷** (Fuguo Haidi Shijie; inside the south gate of the Workers' Stadium; tel: 6591 3397; 8am–6.30pm; charge), supposedly the largest aquarium

of its kind in Beijing. The **Beijing Zoo** (137 Xizhimenwai Dajie; tel: 6831 4411; daily 7.30am–5pm) in western Beijing also has an aquarium; however, the popularity of the zoo ensures that on any day nice enough to visit, a substantial percentage of the city will be there ahead of you. The Blue Zoo promises a far less harrowing experience.

The Blue Zoo aquarium sports a 3.5 million-litre tank of artificial sea water that forms a walk-through aquarium supporting a complete mini-ecosystem of sea creatures. Several smaller tanks hold a variety of other sea life, including sharks. Shark feeding shows are put on twice daily and snorkelling and scuba lessons can be taken when instructors are available.

Above: children can have a jolly good time in Beijing.

Underwater Fun
The Blue Zoo is a popular spot for all kinds of underwater activities – even underwater marriages are regularly held here.

Below: the Blue Zoo is a sanctuary for many kinds of marine creatures.

RITAN PARK

From Gongren Tiyuchang Nanlu, walk south for 20 minutes, or take a taxi if time is short. South of Chaoyangmenwai Dajie is **Ritan Park ③** (Ritan Gongyuan; daily 6am–9pm; free). Originally built in 1530, Ritan, the Altar of the Sun, was one of a set of eight altars, including Ditan, Yuetan, Shejitan and Tiantan (dedicated to the earth, moon, crops and heaven, respectively), which emperors would visit on set dates to make offerings to the powers of the cosmos. Ritan was used on the spring equinox, when emperors observed a ritual of changing clothes at the Dressing Hall, and sacrifices were brought from the Divine Depot and the Divine Kitchen to the Slaughter Pavilion.

Ritan Park, one of the oldest parks in the city, is also one of the most peaceful and pleasant. Its northern half is taken up by historical buildings and a few small museums and monuments. The atmosphere is tranquil, and made more so by the elderly people who come here to sing, exercise and fly kites.

Young children will like the southern end of the park more. There is a small amusement park with merry-go-rounds and other rides, as well as a small monorail, for which per-entry tickets can be purchased. A large fish pond is kept stocked with carp and other edible fish, and fishing poles can be rented by the half-hour. Another small lake is equipped with small remote-controlled boats (or ice-sleds when it is frozen over in winter), which are the only real disturbance to the peace. And if you bring your young ones to Ritan Park on a nice weekend, there will be numerous other local children, who will be happy to welcome them into their games.

There are no lack of dining options in this part of town, though since this is an embassy district there is a higher-than-average concentration of Western options. If you fancy Cantonese food on a pleasant deck outside, then head out of the south gate and turn right to find **La Galerie**, see ⑪①. For children who are fussy eaters or if you simply fancy something simple, consider burgers and milkshakes at **Grandma's Kitchen**, see ⑪②, further south or reliable pizza and pasta at **Annie's** Italian restaurant, see ⑪③, within the Ritan Highlife development opposite the north gate.

Imported Western snacks suitable for a picnic can be found at **Jenny Lou's**, see ⑪④. The area is in fact full of restaurants – stroll down Guanghua Lu or Ritan Lu further south for more choices.

Lastly, if your child is experiencing any health problem, this is also the place to come to. The **Bayley and Jackson Medical Centre** (tel: 8562 9998; www.bjhealthcare.com) on Ritan Donglu has a paediatrics centre, with doctors who are fluent in English.

Above: kite-flying is a popular sport in Ritan Park.

Below: parents and children take a breather in Ritan Park.

Food and Drink 🍴

① LA GALERIE
Just west of Ritan Park south gate; tel: 8562 8698; daily 10am–10.30pm; $$$
This long-standing Cantonese restaurant is a reliable option with pleasant outdoor seating and a particularly good lunchtime dim sum menu.

② GRANDMA'S KITCHEN
11 Xiushui Nanjie; tel: 6503 2893; daily 7.30am–11pm; $$
When it has been a long slog through China and the kids have gone on hunger strike, Grandma's Kitchen may be your only recourse. American-style burgers, thick shakes and skillet scrambles, served in a down-home atmosphere just on the far side of kitsch, ought to restore the spirits of the most recalcitrant little troopers.

③ ANNIE'S
Unit 9, Ritan High Life, 39 Shenlu Jie; tel: 8569 3031; daily 11am–11pm; $$
Simple, Italian American food including pizza and a family friendly atmosphere that even extends to special play areas for the little ones.

④ JENNY LOU'S
4 Ritan Beilu; tel: 8563 0626; daily 8am–midnight; $–$$
One of a chain of import supermarkets, Jenny Lou's caters to foreigners, Westerners in particular, who are looking for a taste of home. Sliced bread, cold cuts, sausage rolls, cakes, fruit juices and canned drinks are all available.

OLD AND NEW BEIJING

Beijing is one of the oldest – and fastest-changing – capitals in the world. This walk moves from the Central Business District, the city's most modern sector, to some of its oldest neighbourhoods, revealing the ways in which the past and the future intermesh.

DISTANCE 7½km (5½ miles)

TIME A full day

START World Trade Center

END New Poly Plaza

POINTS TO NOTE

Start from the Guomao subway stop. After exploring the CBD, either walk to Jinbao Jie, or take the subway to the Jianguomen stop, and head north from there to Dongsi Shitiao.

The heart of Beijing's new downtown is the **World Trade Center ❶**, also known as Guomao. This part of town was still farmland when Guomao was built in the late 1980s, but a combination of market forces and energetic city planning has turned this area into the economic heart of the modern capital. The CBD (Central Business District) now occupies an area of roughly 4 sq km (1½ sq miles) and it is set to double in size by 2017.

Designs by 'Starchitects'

The issue of foreign architects carrying out projects in Beijing is one of some controversy. Rem Koolhaas' CCTV Tower, Paul Andreu's National Grand Theatre, PTW's National Aquatics Centre and Herzog & de Meuron's National Stadium are seen by some as badges of Beijing's cosmopolitanism, by others as a kind of cultural invasion – architects playing with outré designs no other country would accept.

NEW BUSINESS DISTRICT

The jewel in the crown of the CBD is the **China Central Television Station Tower** ❷ (Zhongyang Dianshitai; CCTV), just across Dongsanhuan Lu from Guomao. The tower was conceived by international superstar architect Rem Koolhaas, and built for a rumoured €850 million. It was designed with an industrial workflow in mind – one 'leg' is devoted to broadcasting, the other to research and planning, and the joining section at the top houses management.

Beginning from the CCTV Tower, wander at will in the CBD. The **China World Trade Center Tower III** is Beijing's tallest building at 330m (1,083ft) a number you can appreciate from the 80th floor at Atmosphere Bar see ⑨①. South of the World Trade Center, the uniform, boxlike home/office complex **Jianwai SOHO** is hard to miss. Built by Chinese 'starchitect' Pan Shiyi, the iconic design will doubtlessly shape the blueprint of the future CBD.

SILK MARKET

If the weather is nice and it is early, stroll down Guanghua Lu from the CBD to Erhuan Lu (Second Ring Road). This leafy neighbourhood is one of Beijing's two embassy districts, and is surprisingly peaceful despite its location in the middle of town. On your way, pop into the **Silk Market** ❸ (Xiushui Shichang), home to

Above from far left: Guomao, the World Trade Center; the landmark CCTV tower;Jianwai SOHO's distinctive facade.

Real Estate Mogul

Pan Shiyi might be the only household name in the Beijing real estate industry. His story is impressive: beginning as a poor peasant in Gansu province, Pan gradually worked his way into the construction and real estate business, and after making a small fortune in Hainan he descended on Beijing in the early 1990s. He built offices and apartments in primary colours instead of the government-mandated grey, and vigorously marketed his projects – all revolutionary for the time. The CBD was completed in Pan's imagination practically before a single building was standing, and his vision and daring have goaded a conservative industry into breathtaking action. Of course, complaints abound. His aggressive marketing tactics have helped drive prices sky-high, and he is a shameless self-promoter (negotiations to star in a Chinese version of Donald Trump's *The Apprentice* dragged on for years). There are also grumbles that, in the supremely corrupt real estate industry, its leading man could not have kept his hands clean. But there is no doubt that Pan and his SOHO projects have changed the face of modern Beijing.

Food and Drink

① ATMOSPHERE BAR
80th Floor, China World Trade Centre Tower III; tel: 6505 2299
The views from Beijing's tallest building are, unsurprisingly, impressive. Part of the Shangri-la Hotel, this lounge bar does in fact manage a decent atmosphere. Expensive but excellent cocktails and Japanese whiskies pad out the drinks menu.

First Paved Street
Dongzongbu Hutong was the first street in all of Beijing to be paved, in 1913.

Courtyard Homes
Nostalgia for old courtyard homes is sometimes misplaced: though most have running water, few have internal plumbing. Washing up is done in highly unsanitary public toilets. Poor electrical wiring, crumbling roofs, rats and cockroaches all help detract from the atmosphere.

Below: an equatorial armilla at the Beijing Ancient Observatory.

brand-name counterfeit goods. You can also choose to take the subway from Yong'anli to Jianguomen.

ANCIENT OBSERVATORY

At the junction of Jianguomennei and the Second Ring Road is the **Ancient Observatory** ❹ (Gu Guangxiangtai). Originally constructed in 1279 north of its present-day site, the observatory that you see today was built in the mid-15th century and sits atop a watchtower that was once part of the city walls. It served both the Ming and Qing dynasties in making predications based on astrology, as well as helping navigators who were about to go to sea. It remains an evocative reminder of the era in which Jesuit priests advised Chinese emperors, and

reading the stars was of crucial importance to governance.

ZONGBU HUTONG

Not far from the Jianguomen subway stop is **Dongzongbu Hutong** ❺, leading west from Jianguomen Beidajie. The three sections of **Zongbu Hutong** are some of the oldest-surviving streets in Beijing, dating back at least 600 years. Foreign ambassadors lived here during the invasion of the European Eight Allied Armies in the late 19th century, and negotiations between the Communists, Nationalists and Americans during China's civil war also took place here.

From here, you can continue on to **Xizongbu Hutong** and explore the old buildings; otherwise, find the entrance to **Beizongbu Hutong** and head north. At the northern end of the alleyway, on the right, is the **former residence of Liang Sicheng**. During the 1920s and 1930s, the intellectual and his wife Lin Huiyin held a cultural salon here, which was attended by many of the greatest artists and reform-minded thinkers of the day.

Go further west to Chaoyangmen Nanxiaojie, cross the street to the west side, and head north from there. On the east side of the street are the so-called *weigai* apartment blocks, areas where ostensibly dangerous courtyard houses have been replaced with six- or eight-storey apartment blocks. On the west side are the old, untouched neighbourhoods, with tree-shaded lanes winding back among the courtyards, filled with bicycles and people.

If it is time for lunch, there is plenty of simple street food in this area, plus a wealth of restaurants. One excellent choice is **Qin Tang Fu**, see ⑪②, serving authentic Shaanxi noodles. Otherwise, proceed further past Chaoyangmennei Dajie to find even more choices *(see below)*.

'Haunted' House

Continue north on Chaoyangmen Nanxiaojie onto Chaoyangmen Beixiaojie. As you pass Chaoyangmennei Dajie, head a few hundred metres/yards east where, on the north side of the road, an old, ivy-covered building sits back from the road. Built around the turn of the last century, this building was said to have been bestowed by the emperor on British residents for use as a church, but was more likely used as a foreign mission. It is one of the most famous 'haunted' houses of Beijing today – supposedly a Nationalist Army officer's wife hung herself in one of the rooms.

DONGSI SHITIAO

Return to the north-south route. The alleyways running off Chaoyangmen Nanxiaojie all have names based on their historical usage; those further north are known as **Dongsi Shitiao** (Ten Alleys of Dongsi) and are called by their numbers. These names have remained the same since the Ming dynasty, except for a brief period during the Cultural Rev-

olution when they were known as the '18 Alleys of Red Sun Street'.

Further north in Dongsi Liutiao (Alley Six) is the Xinjiang restaurant **Crescent Moon** (Wanwan Yueliang), see ⑪③. If you're in the mood for more than a simple dinner later tonight, make a reservation at the **Red Capital Club**, see ⑪④, well in advance.

NANXINCANG

Turn right onto the street of **Dongsi Shitiao ❻** (sometimes called Ping'an Dajie) and head towards Erhuan Lu (Chaoyangmen Beidajie/Chaoyangmen Nandajie). Before you reach Dongsi Shitiao Bridge, you will see a cluster of

Above from far left: jewellery and handbags at the Silk Market; view of *hutong* housing.

Food and Drink

② QIN TANG FU
69 Chaoyangmen Nanxiaojie; tel: 6559 8135; daily 11am–2pm and 5–10pm; $
Saozimian (sister-in-law's noodles) is the thing to get, or branch out for spicy mutton dumplings and pork sandwiches. Try a mug of the sweet white *choujiu* – a mild rice-based alcoholic drink – or sour plum juice. The dolls, paper cut wall hangings, and knee-high tables are all typical of Shaanxi culture.

③ CRESCENT MOON
16 Dongsi Liutiao (Alley Six), about 100m/yds in from Chaoyangmen Beixiaojie; tel: 6400 5281; daily 10am–11.30pm; $
This is a few notches more authentic than most Xinjiang restaurants in Beijing. The food, such as mutton skewers (*yangrou chuan'r*) and 'big-plate chicken' (*da pan'r ji*), comes in Xinjiang-sized portions.

④ RED CAPITAL CLUB
66 Dongsi Jiutiao (Alley Nine); tel: 8401 6152;
www.redcapitalclub.com.cn; daily 6pm–midnight; $$$
Ostensibly for the 'new red capitalists', this trades on its Mao-era memorabilia and atmosphere, offering a slice of privileged life as China's top leaders might have lived it. Thus the plush surroundings, Red Flag limos, and an impressive cigar selection. The cuisine is 'Zhongnanhai' – you'll eat what the Chinese leaders eat.

Above from left:
fresh produce in
Dongsi Shitiao;
shaobing (griddle-fried
cakes) is a familiar
street snack; National
Stadium; song and
dance at the Ethnic
Culture Park.

Hutong Names
Some of the more
colourful alleyway
names include:
Yanyue ('performing
music') Hutong,
which once housed
music schools and
teachers; Shijia
Hutong, which was
named for a
powerful family who
lived there; and
Ganmian Hutong,
where dried noodles
were once sold.

old-looking buildings on the south side
of the street. During the Ming and
Qing dynasties, these were the *huang-
jia liangcang* – imperial granaries that
stored food for emperors and their
immediate families, ensuring that
famine would never harm royalty. These
old buildings have been remodelled and
opened for limited use, and are now
known as **Nanxincang ❼**. Though it
had made many preservationists anx-
ious, the re-use of the imperial granaries
is now generally seen as a success. Strict
rules governing the treatment of the old
buildings were put in place by experts
(not officials) and, more surprisingly,
enforced. This little area has since
become a hip nightlife district. Three
granary buildings are given over to the
Xin Beijing Art Gallery; others house
fancy restaurants, bars and clubs. An
excellent dinner option here is **Dadong
Peking Duck Restaurant**, see ❶⑤. If
you are looking for a more modest,
down-to-earth meal, cross the street

north of the granaries to **Fu Jia Lou**, see
❶⑥, a traditional Beijing eatery.

POLY PLAZAS

Situated kitty-corner from each other,
across Dongsi Shitiao Bridge, are the
old and new Poly plazas. In some
ways, they stand for the great leap
that Beijing's architecture has made in
the past 20 years. The **Old Poly Plaza
❽** (Baoli Dasha) is painted a drab
yellow colour and houses the Poly
Theatre *(see Entertainment, p.19)*. The
New Poly Plaza ❾ (Xinbaoli Dasha),
built by the US architectural firm
SOM, is monumental without being
overbearing, composed of an interesting combination of glass curtain
walls and subtly coloured metal
plating. The ninth floor is home to
the Poly Art Museum.

Poly Museum

If it is not too late in the day, visit the
Poly Museum (Baoli Yishu Bowuguan; tel: 6500 1188; Mon–Sat
9.30am–4.30pm; charge). Only a
small part of the Poly Group's collection is on view, but every piece is a
treasure. The main room features
Buddha statues dating back to the
Tang dynasty, and the exhibition
design is masterful – the room
hushed, each statue lit with a spot-
light, the air of antiquity palpable.
Further on are a few bronze heads of
the twelve animals of the Chinese
zodiac (*shengxiao*), which were looted
from the Old Summer Palace (Yuanmingyuan).

Food and Drink 🍴

⑤ DADONG PEKING DUCK
G/F, Nanxincang Office Towers; tel: 5169 0329; daily
11am–10pm; $$$
One of the best places in town for Peking duck. All Dadong
chain restaurants are appallingly popular, so make a reservation
at least a day in advance. Dadong is also known for duck
dishes such as duck liver pate and duck soups.

⑥ FU JIA LOU
23 Dongsi Shitiao Dajie; tel: 8403 7831; daily 11am–2pm and
4.30–9.30pm; $
Zhajiangmian, a rice-noodle dish with fermented bean sauce, is a
feature of the Beijing cuisine here, as are various tofu and bean-
paste snacks. The main attraction is the incredible din: the louder
the merrier, with plates clashing and waitstaff shouting.

THE OLYMPIC PARK

The city planners went to great lengths to beautify the areas around the awe-inspiring facilities for the 2008 Olympics. This tour brings you to the Olympic sights and Beijing's enormous forest park, the best way to escape the crowds, plus an ancient city wall and the Chinese Ethnic Culture Park.

The grand Olympic designs remain a monument to the excesses of the games. Virtually unused as sporting grounds, they serve as landmarks of a new, ambitious China and top tourist sites.

TUCHENG PARK

The 4.8km (3-mile) -long **Tucheng Park ①** (Tucheng Gongyuan), your first stop, was once part of the city wall

---

DISTANCE 4½km (2¾ miles)
TIME Half a day, or a full day if you linger in the forest park
START Tucheng Park
END Olympic Forest Park
POINTS TO NOTE
Take the subway to the Beitucheng subway stop. It's worth checking ahead if any special events or performances are taking place at the Olympic stadiums.

---

of Dadu, the capital of the Yuan dynasty. The wall was originally made of earth (*tucheng* means 'earthen wall'); only a few shapeless mounds remain, but the city moat, called Little Moon River (*Xiaoyuehe*), still exists.

ETHNIC CULTURE PARK

The **Chinese Ethnic Culture Park ②** (Minzuyuan; 1 Minzuyuan Lu; tel: 6206 3647; daily 8.30am–6pm; charge) showcases the various architectural and living styles of the 56 ethnic groups of China, including the majority Han. Typical dwellings of various ethnic minorities – from the Tibetans' inward-sloping forts to the slate-piled houses of the Bouyei – have been transported here

Xanadu
The 'Xanadu' mentioned in Samuel Taylor Coleridge's poem *Kubla Khan* is in fact a real location, referring to Shangdu, a summer palace of the Yuan emperors, originally located north and west of present-day Beijing.

Ethnic Groups
That there are precisely 56 ethnic groups in China is something laid down in the early days of the PRC. Though many groups would be better split into two or even three, the number 56 has become politically non-negotiable.

Above from left:
inside the National
Stadium; National
Aquatics Centre; 798
is the perfect place
for an art-gallery
crawl; signage at the
entrance to 798.

from their native areas. Members of the various ethnicities have also been hired to represent their people in traditional dress. In this sense, visitors can gain a crash course on the various groups.

Though the minorities are each given a display that details their particular crafts, customs and beliefs, the emphasis always returns to cultural shows with singing and dancing, even if these activities do not figure much in some cultures. Be warned: the shows can be painfully condescending and tacky.

Between the northern and southern sections of the park are a few restaurants serving ethnic food. Among them, **Caixianggen**, see ⑪①, serves authentic Hunanese food.

OLYMPIC FACILITIES

Along with the chance to host the 2008 Olympics Games, Beijing also won the chance to have a makeover with some world-class architectural projects.

National Stadium

Head north from the Ethnic Culture Park and you come to the 3.5 billion-yuan **National Stadium** ❸ (Guojia Tiyuchang), designed by the Swiss firm Herzog & de Meuron. Its main feature are the girders that function as both structure and facade – the building is essentially a steel network completely open to the elements. It's also open to tourists, and is one of Beijing's top attractions.

National Aquatics Centre

The **National Aquatics Centre** ❹

(Guojia Youyong Zhongxin; tel: 8437 1588; www.water-cube.com; daily 9am–7pm; charge), designed by the PTW architectural firm from Sydney, was inspired by the work of two Irish physicists on the structure of soap bubbles. Its walls are made of steel girders draped with a teflon-like material, which is inflated with pumps. The transparent walls trap most of the energy from sunlight, providing a natural source of heating for the pools. The centre houses a water park and fitness facilities.

Olympic Forest Park

The **Olympic Forest Park** ❺ (Aolinpike Senlin Gongyuan), north of the sports facilities, is the city's largest green space. Positioned on the same north-south axis that runs through the Forbidden City and the Drum Tower, the 12¼-sq-km (5-sq-mile) park is a carefully constructed expanse of woods, lakes and meandering pathways with a bird reserve in the northern section and a garden to the south. The central Main Lake can be explored by rented pedalo.

Nicknames
The locals have nicknamed the National Stadium the 'Bird's Nest', while the National Aquatics Centre is known as the 'Water Cube'.

Food and Drink

① CAIXIANGGEN

8 Minzuyuan Lu; tel: 6680 4025; daily 11am–2pm and 5pm till late; $$
Hunan is Chairman Mao's place of birth, and most Hunanese restaurants advertise themselves as serving 'Mao food'. Not Caixianggen, which forgoes some of the spicier, oilier dishes beloved by Mao in favour of greater variety. Recommended are the radish and beef stew, bacon and bamboo root, and donkey meat, which is surprisingly tender.

MODERN ART

Since the turn of the century, Beijing's modern art scene has seen not only a vast proliferation of artists, but also widespread recognition from international art circles. This new renown has transformed Chinese art markets and also Beijing's art-viewing experience.

Luckily for art enthusiasts, the vast majority of Beijing's modern art is concentrated in one area of town. The neighbourhood, called **Dashanzi**, is an old military factory district, a remnant of the early days of the PRC. The factories and warehouses here have partially been converted into artists' studios and galleries, while heavy machinery is still chugging right next to the photography exhibitions and performance art.

The first artists arrived here in 2001–2, including the designer Huang Rui, who is in some ways the artists' patron saint. In 2002, the inaugural art show was held, following which more artists flocked here to establish studios. At that

---

DISTANCE 2km (1¼ miles)

TIME A full day

START 798 Art District

END Caochangdi

POINTS TO NOTE

A taxi is more or less the only option here. Taxi drivers are becoming more aware of the 798 Art District, but you may have to direct your driver to Dashanzi Huandao and then north from there on to 798 on Jiuxianqiao Beilu. It is possible to walk from 798 to Caochangdi (half an hour), but it's far more pleasant to take a taxi. Note that most 798 Art District galleries are closed on Mondays.

Buying Art

Beijing was once an excellent place to buy breathtaking pieces of art for a song, but no more. International attention has driven prices to international levels – good for the artists, no doubt, but hard on local art markets. Expect prices to be quoted in US dollars.

Above from left:
gallery of 798 Space;
798 Photo Gallery;
exhibition at Beijing
Tokyo Art Projects;
Timezone 8
bookstore.

time, the rent was as low as 0.1 yuan per square metre per day. By 2004, however, rental had gone up considerably more, and in recent years artists' studios have largely been taken over by internationally funded galleries as well as fancy restaurants and cafés.

Bauhaus Chic

In the early days of the PRC, the country received a great deal of technical assistance from abroad, particularly from the Soviet Union. 798 (originally known as Factory 718) was the first major project undertaken with the help of the East Germans, instead of the Soviets. The factory was meant to manufacture radio components, and the Soviets, who themselves imported this technology from the Germans, told the Chinese to go straight to the source. Built at a cost of nearly 150 million yuan, the factory was one of the largest projects in Beijing at that time. The Germans originally intended to design the buildings with local characteristics, as they had in Russia, but the Chinese, wanting to ensure success, told them to build as they did at home in Germany. The result is the unique Bauhaus look, best exemplified by the main 798 Space building – with saw-toothed roofs and lots of window space. The windows face north (counter to Chinese tradition) because the northern light is indirect, casting fewer distracting shadows on the machinery. Coincidentally, the same principal makes for excellent art-viewing conditions.

798 ART DISTRICT

This tour begins at the 798 Art District. When the factories were built, in the early 1950s, they were numbered, rather than named. Although the art district has expanded to include the 781 area to the north, the name 798 has remained.

There is essentially a square kilometre of space here in which to wander freely. As you enter through the front gate, check out the large red map on the right-hand side, which will help you locate the galleries. There is another map on the main road further in. Public toilets are available here, but they are not always sanitary; it might be easier to visit one in a café or restaurant. Most factories that are still in operation are clearly marked and can hence be easily avoided.

Otherwise, there is art of one sort or another to be found in the countless galleries and venues in 798 – the area can easily provide a weekend's worth of sights. The following are some of the better-known venues:

❶ 798 Space
Tel: 6437 6248
www.798space.com
Daily 10.30am–7.30pm
This is one of the main venues in 798 for large-scale international exhibitions and the first space set up by Huang Rui and photographer Xu Yong, in 2002. It also hosts fashion shows and the annual Dashanzi International Art Festival.

❷ Ullens Centre for Contemporary Art

Tel: 8459 9269

www.ucca.org.cn

Daily 10am–6pm

A multi-million dollar not-for-profit exhibition space that sets itself apart by hosting impressive, free exhibitions and allowing visitors to take photographs.

❸ 798 Photo Gallery

Tel: 6438 1784

www.798photogallery.cn

Daily 10am–6pm

This gallery consistently shows some of the best and most provocative photography in the 798 Art District. From shocking pictures of the Cultural Revolution to the latest meditations on consumer culture in China, there is always something worth seeing.

❹ Long March Space

Tel: 6438 7107

www.longmarchspace.com

Daily 11am–7pm

One of the most active galleries in the area, Long March's success is mostly due to the curatorial vision of Lu Jie, who is one of the most internationally involved artist-curators in 798. He has arranged travelling art exhibitions in China and residencies for foreign artists.

❺ Timezone 8

Tel: 8456 0336

www.timezone8.com

Daily 11am–8pm

American Robert Bernell was the first foreigner to move into 798 in 2001. This bookstore is far and away the best art-related bookshop in the city, carrying foreign art and photography books, international art magazines and tomes of local artists' works. It is part of a Hong Kong-based publishing company run by Bernell, which puts out art-related volumes, including the definitive book on 798, *Beijing 798*.

For lunch or light refreshments, try **AT Café**, see Ⓨ①, for trendy fusion fare, or the **Timezone 8 Café**, see Ⓨ②, for something simpler.

CAOCHANGDI

If the 798 Art District is too commercial for your artistic sensibilities there is also **Caochangdi**, a smaller art area

Above: Long March Space; Beijing Tokyo Art Projects; AT Café.

Food and Drink 🍴

① AT CAFÉ

4 ,Jiuxianqiao Lu; tel: 6438 7204, daily 10am–midnight; $$

This hip little eatery offers a small menu of pasta dishes, pastries and simple Chinese fare, along with a modest selection of wines and cocktails. With the same 'industrial chic' decor that characterises all of 798, it is a great spot to meet friends, catch glimpses of famous artists, or simply watch tourists go by.

② TIMEZONE 8 CAFÉ

4 Jiuxianqiao Lu; tel: 8456 0336; daily 8.30am–9pm; $

Part of the Timezone 8 bookstore, this café offers a wide variety of drinks – coffee, Chinese tea and fruit juices – along with light meal options such as salads, sandwiches and pastries. With its free Wi-fi, or with a book from the bookstore, this is an ideal spot to while away an afternoon.

Above from left:
Chinese contemporary art at China Art Archives and Warehouse; Platform China; Temple of the Azure Clouds; statue of Sun Yat-sen at the Sun Yat-sen Memorial Hall.

not too far to the north. This satellite district came into being thanks to one of the great, and most controversial, figures of Beijing's art scene, Ai Weiwei. The son of a famous poet named Ai Qing, Ai Weiwei was a member of The Stars, one of the earliest art movements formed following the end of the Cultural Revolution. After more than a decade in the United States, Ai Weiwei returned to Beijing and began a career as an art icon. His China Art Archives and Warehouse (CAAW) opened in Caochangdi in 2000, when the area was just farmland, but it has since attracted enough satellite venues to join it, making Caochangdi a district in its own right.

Caochangdi is not an easy area to negotiate. Walking here from 798 is possible, although not too pleasant – the walk is mostly along a highway. Taxi drivers may know of Caochangdi, but it is better to call a gallery and have the staff give directions to the driver.

Here are two worthwhile locations:

❻ China Art Archives and Warehouse
Tel: 8456 5152
www.archivesandwarehouse.com
Wed–Sun 2–6pm
This original Caochangdi venue has hosted many ground-breaking exhibitions, mostly featuring Ai Weiwei's friends – meaning some of the top experimental artists in China.

❼ Platform China
Tel: 6432 0169
www.platformchina.org
Tue–Sun 11am–6pm
As much a communications and art-exchange organisation as it is a gallery, this facilitates exchanges within and outside China, and also provides artist residencies. The gallery's focus is cutting-edge works by Chinese artists, including video and new media.

Below: the spacious gallery of Platform China.

FRAGRANT HILLS PARK

The temples and pavilions of the Fragrant Hills Park, located north-west of the city, are a popular hiking destination and offer excellent views of the city on clear days.

DISTANCE 3km (1½ miles)
TIME Half a day
START Temple of the Azure Clouds
END Beijing Botanical Gardens
POINTS TO NOTE
This walk involves some hilly, though not difficult, terrain, so wear strong shoes and get an early start. And if the weather permits, this is a good opportunity for a picnic lunch. There is also an option for a boat tour at the Summer Palace. From the city centre, take a taxi (around 50 yuan) or a bus (No. 714, 318, 331 or 904). Expect the journey to take an hour or more.

The **Fragrant Hills Park** (Xiangshan Gongyuan; daily, summer 6am–7pm, winter 6am–6pm; charge) was a favourite hunting retreat of emperors from the 12th to 18th centuries. A number of emperors made their mark here by building pagodas and temples. At the height of its popularity, during the Qing emperor Qianlong's reign, the walled park was filled with exotic deer. Mao Zedong lived here briefly in 1949, at Shuangqing Villa, before he moved to Zhongnanhai next to the Forbidden City. Much of the Fragrant Hills Park fell into decay or was destroyed by European armies between 1860 and 1900, but it has since been restored and is now one of the most popular destinations for day trippers from Beijing, particularly in the autumn.

TEMPLE OF THE AZURE CLOUDS

The park's ticket office is just left of the main entrance. Once inside, follow the stone path that veers right and buy another ticket to visit the **Temple of the Azure Clouds** ❶ (Biyunsi; daily 8am–5pm; charge).

A temple was first built here in 1330 and later generations added new buildings, especially during the Qing dynasty. The first hall contains two huge celestial guardians, and the second has a statue of the Maitreya Buddha, all from the Ming dynasty. The innermost hall is the **Sun Yat-sen Memorial Hall** (Sun Zhongshan Jiniantang), in memory of the leader of the Nationalist movement that overthrew the Qing dynasty. To the right of his statue is a crystal coffin, a rather macabre gift from the Soviet Union.

One of the temple's more unusual treasures is the Indian-style 35m (115ft) **Diamond Throne Pagoda** at the rear of the complex. On the first level is a sanctuary with carved monster heads.

Good Luck Charms
Visitors to the Temple of the Azure Clouds write their names on pennants to ask for blessings.

Choose Your Day Wisely
On nice weekend days, there can be so many people at the Fragrant Hills Park that it becomes literally impossible to return via public transport.

**Off the
Beaten Track**
The mountainside is
riddled with small
paths and forgotten
temples. If you're
not in a hurry,
exploration is
guaranteed to
be rewarding.

This held Sun Yat-sen's body from 1925 to 1929 before it was moved to Nanjing. Climb up the inner stairs to the top terrace, with its central tower surrounded by six small pagodas covered in carved bodhisattvas (enlightened beings).

After descending and passing the Sun Yat-sen Memorial Hall, on your right is the impressive **Hall of 500 Luohan** (500 Luohantang). Enter through the side gate in the lower terrace of this courtyard. The gilded wooden statues (508 in all) represent legendary senior monks (*luohan*) who achieved a higher insight into Buddhist truth and moral duty. Some of the statues meditate peacefully, one has a lion springing from his chest, and an old monk tears off his skin to reveal the face of a young man.

INCENSE BURNER PEAK

Walk down the hill from the temple the same way you came but turn right into Fragrant Hills Park proper just before you reach the exit. Another name for Fragrant Hills is **Incense Burner Peak ❷** (Xianglufeng), a description of its appearance when fog settles on the 557m (1,827ft) high summit. About 50m/yds along the path on the right is the ticket office for the cable car (daily 8.30am–5pm), which substitutes a 15-minute ride for an hour's steep climb. On the right is the Diamond Throne Pagoda again; to the left is **Spectacles Lake** (Yanjinghu), named for its resemblance to a pair of spectacles, and beyond is the white glow of the luxurious Fragrant Hills Hotel.

After admiring the view from the pavilion on the summit, you have two choices. You can take the cable car back to the bottom and head southwards, visiting Spectacles Lake and the **Temple of Clarity** (Zhaomiao). Pass the east gate (but do not exit), walk several hundred metres/yards along a leafy path that exits onto the main road leading to the Fragrant Hills Hotel. Turn right and walk 150m/yds to the hotel's main entrance.

If you have more energy, descend using the path down from the Incense Burner Peak, starting at the end of the pavilion furthest from the cable car terminus. The pleasant path zigzags through lush forest. On the way down – a 40-minute walk – take the right whenever the path forks. Halfway down, you pass an old hunting lodge, two more pavilions and the ruins of the **Fragrant Hills Temple** ❸ (Xiangshansi), in the clutches of some gnarled pines.

Fragrant Hills Hotel

Just beyond the temple, the path joins a road. Turn left and walk 100m/yds to the main gate of the **Fragrant Hills Hotel** ❹ (Xiangshan Fandian; tel: 6259 1166). This oasis of luxury, designed by Chinese-American architect I.M. Pei, embraces classical Chinese themes, such as terraces, gates within gates and courtyards surrounded by halls, with modern angles and skylights. In the expansive grounds, an elaborately crafted Chinese garden blends into the wooded surroundings.

Maimai Jie, by the Fragrant Hills Hotel, is the main street leading to the front gate of the Fragrant Hills, and a carnival of street food and handicrafts. There is plenty to eat here; one good choice is the café-restaurant **Sculpting in Time**, see

⑪①, a pleasant spot for a coffee and a quick meal, and an alternative to the outside seating at the Fragrant Hills Hotel Café.

Beijing Botanical Gardens

Less physically challenging than the mountaintop is the **Beijing Botanical Gardens** ❺ (Beijing Zhiwuyuan; daily, summer 6am–7pm, winter 7am–5pm; charge) at the foot of the hill about 2km (1¼ miles) from Biyunsi. Great expense has gone into making this a first-class garden, with extensive collections of roses and other flowers from around the world – this is the largest plant collection in China. Beautiful landscaping leads back into hidden paths and glades on the skirts of the mountain. An enormous greenhouse (separate charge) houses tropical plants, and can be a lifesaver during Beijing's cold, dry and dusty winters. Within the grounds is also the former residence of Cao Xueqin (Cao Xueqin Jinianguan), where it is thought Cao wrote the classic novel *Dream of the Red Mansions*.

Above from far left: stone carving at the Diamond Throne Pagoda; Spectacles Lake; entrance to the Temple of Clarity; roof ornament at the Fragrant Hills Park.

Souvenirs
The traditional Fragrant Hills souvenir is a handful of red autumn leaves, pressed, dried and vacuum-sealed.

Sal Tree Stele
The Qing emperor Qianlong wrote the inscription of the Sal Tree Stele at the Fragrant Hills Temple, which he visited in 1773 and 1785. The inscription was carved in Sanskrit, Manchu, Mongolian and Han languages.

THE MING TOMBS AND THE GREAT WALL AT MUTIANYU

An excursion that combines a rich encounter with Ming-dynasty history at the Ming Tombs, a beautiful drive through the mountains and an afternoon hike on the spectacular Great Wall at Mutianyu.

Above: various figures stand guard along the Avenue of Stone Figures.

Right: the Ming tombs are nestled in a natural amphitheatre that is considered good for *feng shui.*

DISTANCE 49km (30 miles). The Ming Tombs are 50km (30 miles) northwest of Beijing; the Great Wall at Mutianyu is 75km (45 miles) northeast of Beijing.

TIME A full day

START The Ming Tombs

END The Great Wall at Mutianyu

POINTS TO NOTE

Consider hiring a taxi for the day to take in both major sites. Otherwise, take the subway to Nanshao station then a 10km (6-mile) taxi journey to Dagongmen to see the Ming Tombs. Tourist buses from Qianmen or Dongzhimen ply the Ming Tombs route, often making impromptu stops. Expect vigorous walking and climbing.

Although Beijing was the capital of of five dynasties, only the tombs of Ming emperors are in relatively close proximity to the capital.

Thirteen of the 16 Ming emperors who reigned from 1368 to 1644 are buried about 50km (30 miles) north-west of Beijing, in an amphitheatre formed by mountains on three sides. The foothills of the Yanshan Mountains form a natural entrance to the 40-sq-km (15-sq-mile) basin protected on both sides by the Dragon and Tiger Mountains, which are said to keep harmful winds away from the holy ground.

Heading north from Deshengmen Gate in the city, you retrace the route taken by the imperial dead to their final resting place. About 40km (25 miles) outside the city, you pass through **Changping**, formerly a garrison town that was partly responsible for guarding the tombs. The town has a monument to the peasant leader Li Zicheng, who led the uprising that toppled the Ming dynasty in 1644.

THE MING TOMBS

When you reach the **Ming Tombs** (Shisanling; daily 8.30am–5pm; charge), enter through the **Spirit Way** (Shendao), the path over which the dead were carried during the funeral ceremony. It begins with a white stone portico a few kilometres north of Changping and stretches nearly 6km (4 miles) to the gate of the central tomb. The entrance to the imperial graveyard, which covers 15½ sq km (6 sq miles), is 500m/yds beyond the portico at the **Great Palace Gate** (Dagongmen).

Avenue of Stone Figures

Just beyond the gate is the entrance to the 7km (4-mile) **Avenue of Stone Figures ❶** (Shixiangshendao), also known as the Avenue of Ghosts. It is best to leave your taxi here, and later, rather than paying for a taxi to wait for you, you can catch one of the public buses that leaves from a middle school down Kangfu Lu, just before you reach the Dragon and Phoenix Gate (Longfengmen). The entire tomb complex is built according to exacting principles of Chinese geomancy, or *feng shui*, and this is well illustrated here. Looking through the archway at the southern end of the Spirit Way, you can see that it has been built to perfectly frame the mountains to the west. In fact,

most doorways and archways here have been constructed with the view of what lies beyond them. Go through the archways to reach the avenue, which is lined with statues. Experts still debate the symbolism of these 24 carved stone creatures. Two of these, the *xiezhi* and *qilin*, are two varieties of the Chinese unicorn – mythical animals that may have been placed there for luck. The more familiar elephants, camels and horses are probably meant to serve the emperors in the afterlife. Beyond the animals are 12 stone human statues: four fierce-looking soldiers, four officials and four scholars.

Three of the 13 tombs in this area are officially open as tourist sites: Dingling, Changling and Zhaoling. This excursion takes you on a tour of all three.

Tomb Styles

Below: strolling on the Avenue of Stone Figures.

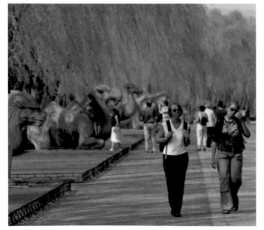

Dingling

Take a bus to **Dingling** ❷ (daily 8.30am–6pm), about 10 minutes from the Avenue of the Stone Figures. Dingling is the burial site of Emperor Wanli, who reigned 1573–1619. Wanli spent eight million silver taels on his bid for immortality, which was enough to feed a million people for 6½ years at the time. It took 30,000 labourers six years to build the subterranean palace of five rooms with graceful arched ceilings – which were full of gold, silver, porcelain and jade treasures at one time.

To reach the vaults, cross the courtyard, climb the **Square Tower** (Fang Cheng) and follow the paths behind. The first room you enter has a pedestal that was intended for Wanli's concubines, but it was mysteriously empty when opened. According to a theory, this room was left empty for fear that repeated opening of the tomb would allow evil winds to disturb Wanli.

The next large room contains three stone altars, which were pushed up against the huge stone-slab doors leading to the room where the coffins of Wanli and his two wives lay along with 26 treasure chests. Some of the treasures are displayed at Changling, your next stop. More lasting is the architectural genius invested in the graves by the Ming emperors. The massive stone doors, now behind glass, were designed such that another stone slab slid into place when closed, locking them from the inside.

Zhaoling

A walkable kilometre southwest from Dingling is **Zhaoling** ❸ (daily 8.30am–5pm), the tomb of Emperor Longqing who reigned 1567–72. Longqing's short rule was characterised by liberal reform that quickly gave way to fulfilling his own personal gratifications. Three empresses were buried with him in what has become a neatly laid-out and quiet spot. Ling'en Hall was used for sacrificial ceremonies and some items remain on display.

Changling

Move on to **Changling** ❹ (daily 8.30am–5.30pm), a five-minute drive north-east of Dingling. The public bus 314 serves the route and runs every 20 minutes from 6.00am–7.40pm. The burial place of Emperor Yongle, who reigned 1403–24, this is the first, largest and best preserved of all the 13 tombs.

According to traditional principles of respect for elder generations, it was in poor taste for the Ming emperors following Yongle to build themselves tombs that was larger than Yongle's, although that did not stop them from doing it. The tomb complex was well tended throughout the Ming dynasty, but the Qing rulers had little motivation to care for the tombs of other dynasties, and the disrepair visible today was mostly incurred during the Qing dynasty.

Changling is a good example of how the tombs were organised. In the front section, a large courtyard dominated by twisted pines leads to a sacrificial hall. The **Hall of Eminent Favours** (Ling'endian) is supported by 32 giant pillars, each carved from a single tree. The dragon-head drains and yellow glazed tiles symbolise imperial majesty. A funeral tablet used to be placed on a wooden altar in the centre of the room, and sacrifices were made before it. The hall now contains an exhibition of items found in Dingling, including jewelled hairpins, suits of armour and the rich dragon brocade used in imperial dress.

The second section of Changling is a courtyard, in which a large stele marks the emperor's grave. Just behind it is the burial mound, enclosed by a wall about 500m/yds long. Presumably, this mound contains Yongle's coffin and burial treasures. To the east and the west are burial grounds for his 16 concubines who, by some accounts, were buried alive, so that they could serve and bring pleasure to Yongle in the next world.

MUTIANYU

In the far corner of the car park in Changling, 100m/yds from the entrance, is a sign in Chinese that says 'Great Wall at Mutianyu 37km'. The drive to the **Great Wall at Mutianyu** ❺ (daily 6.30am–6.30pm; charge, cable car extra) is a beautiful one eastwards through villages and mountains. Mutianyu is slightly further from Beijing than the crowded Badaling section, but it is well worth the journey. As you approach the Great Wall, you pass the **Schoolhouse Canteen**, see ⑪①. If you are feeling peckish, this is the time to stop. If you are taking public transport from the city, board tourist bus 6 from Xuanwumen.

You will spot the Great Wall long before you reach it. Adding together all the sections, the wall extends more than 3,860km (2,400 miles), though some sources may exaggerate its true length, twisting and doubling back from the coast to the north-western province of Gansu. Chinese tourist brochures assert that this is the only man-made structure

Food and Drink 🍴

① SCHOOLHOUSE CANTEEN

Off Jingcheng Expressway, just before Mutianyu (see www.theschool houseatmutianyu.com for map and directions); tel: 6162 6506; daily 10am–6pm; $$
This rather unlikely spot is a full restaurant and folk-arts centre, serving a mix of Italian and Chinese food in beautiful courtyard dining areas. The Schoolhouse can also arrange wall tours, homestays, arts and crafts activities and more. Stop by for a quick lunch before you head up the wall, or linger around for recommendations.

Above from far left: gateway to Changling; statue of Emperor Yongle in the Hall of Eminent Favours; entrance to the Hall of Eminent Favours; inside an underground tomb.

Above: burial paraphernalia on exhibit at Changling.

Above: the cable car provides for an easy ascent, while a luge-like roller coaster leads from the centre of the renovated Mutianyu wall back to the car park.

visible from space (it's rumoured New York's Staten Island garbage dump now shares the honour). Whatever the case, The Great Wall is a terrific lookout point for a soldier, or a tourist.

Rise and Fall of the Wall

The Great Wall is more than a remnant of history. It is also the symbol of the tyranny of imperial rule, the application of mass labour, the ingenuity of engineers and the human desire to build for immortality.

The 'Ten Thousand Li Great Wall', or *Wanli Changcheng* in Mandarin, marked the peak of wall building in China. It is misleading to speak of just one wall. The Great Wall originated as a labyrinth of smaller walls built by warring kingdoms in northern China from 5th century BC. These walls served as fortifications against plundering nomadic tribes from the north. The first Qin emperor, Shi Huangdi, after unifying China in 221BC, made it his mission to link the walls to create a single Great Wall that would defend the country against the nomads. An army of 300,000 labourers is said to have constructed the wall under the leadership of General Meng Tian. In those days, the wall began in the west at Lintao, to the south of Lanzhou, and ran eastwards through the Inner Mongolia, Shaanxi and Hebei provinces, ending in the east of what is now Liaoning.

Wall of Bones

Just as was the case for the Egyptian pyramids, the construction of the wall had its dark, sinister side. Many of the peasants who were conscripted died in the process of wall building. As the many raids and later the full-scale Mongol invasion proved, the wall was only as strong as those who defended it. Nevertheless, once the Yuan dynasty was overthrown, wall building resumed with a vengeance. During the Ming period, the Great Wall really took shape. Mutianyu and most of the other remaining sections date from the Ming dynasty, when the wall was extensively repaired and fortified, and several new sections were added.

Wall Myths

David Spindler is an independent American scholar who has spent the last decade researching the Great Wall full time. He is perhaps the only researcher in the world, Chinese or foreign, dedicated to the study of the Great Wall, and finds himself regularly debunking 'myths' of the wall. Never mind the wall being visible from space or filled with bones, he disputes that no one even knows the real length of the wall, pointing out that previously unknown sections are being discovered all the time. In his view, the wall was quite effective against the Mongols – it was directed against horses more than soldiers. The success of smaller Mongol raids simply proved that for hundreds of years the wall was effective for what it was made for: preventing major mounted invasion.

Climbing Mutianyu

Mutianyu was not part of the main wall but was a barrier shielding passes to the north towards Zhangjiakou. Its high crenellated parapets are part of the Ming-dynasty renovations completed in 1569. The restored Mutianyu section opened in 1986. The steep walk up the wall takes a good 40 minutes, but you can avoid this by taking the cable car and a luge-like slide offers a quick way down. Once on the Wall, a 2.5-km (1.6 miles) restored section leads you across a high ridge, giving views over wooded ravines 90km (55 miles) northeast of Beijing. Mutianyu is notable for its large number of watch-towers and high parapets crenellated for defensive purposes on both sides.

Huanghuacheng and Simatai

Mutianyu is not the only place to climb the wall. A half-hour's drive west of Mutianyu is the section formerly known as the 'Wild Wall', **Huanghuacheng**, which has recently been restored. Much further to the north and the east, nearly in Hebei province, is **Simatai**, which also has a cable car. Simatai shows the unrestored Great Wall at its most majestic, crowning a narrow ridge and sharp pinnacles. To get to Huang-huacheng or Simatai, it is best to join a tour. There are also many other 'unof-ficial' wall sites, though rules forbidding walking on unrenovated sections of the wall have been enforced in recent years.

The journey back to Beijing heads 75km (46 miles) south, entering the city at Dongzhimen.

Above from far left: a pavilion at the Great Wall; tourists climbing the Wall's steep steps.

For Real Men Only
The steepest part of Mutianyu, a 100m/yd stretch that is more like a ladder than a stairway, is called *haohanpo*, or 'real-man slope'.

Below left: the Juyong Pass.

CUANDIXIA

Two-and-a-half hours outside of Beijing city, Cuandixia is one of the best-preserved ancient villages in the greater Beijing area. Dating from the Ming dynasty, it is a remarkably clear window onto the past.

DISTANCE 250km (150 miles) Cuandixia is 90km (56 miles) west of Beijing; the tour itself covers 3–4km (2–2½ miles), depending on how much walking you do.

TIME A full day, or overnight

START AND END You can simply explore the town itself, or head out for longer walks in the hills.

POINTS TO NOTE

Short of driving or taking a very expensive taxi, the best way to and from Cuandixia is by bus. Take the subway to the Pingguoyuan stop, at the end of Line 1. From there, take the twice-daily (7.30am and 12.30pm) bus No. 929 directly to Cuandixia. The bus returns to Beijing at 10am and 3pm. Expect the bus to take about 3 hours each way. Avoid going on a weekend if you don't want to meet too many tourists.

The Hans
The villagers of Cuandixia are mostly surnamed Han, descended from a family that migrated from Shanxi some two hundred years ago.

For a complete change of pace from Beijing's noisy bustle, **Cuandixia** is an excellent choice. This village was built more than 500 years ago, during the Ming Emperor Yongle's reign, and most of its buildings date back to the Ming or Qing dynasties. It is tiny, nestled on a hillside in a narrow pass, and consists of less than a hundred grey stone courtyard homes.

The name Cuandixia means 'below the *cuan*', a *cuan* being a kind of earthen stove, and the horrendously complicated character for this word is written on walls around the village. The character *cuan* (爨) is difficult enough to write that in many cases it is replaced with *chuan* (川 meaning 'river') when referring to the village. You may see the name written in two different ways.

This village was originally a way-station between Beijing and Shanxi province to the west during the Ming dynasty. The trip was once a whole day's ride on a horse, and travellers would stay over in the villagers' homes before continuing their journey. The village was also privileged to supply the imperial palace with goats – goat herders can still be seen in the hills today.

Tranquil Village

While Cuandixia is a tourist destination, it feels remarkably untouristy. There is an entrance fee and a tourist kiosk of sorts, but there are no touts or vendors, and none of the sense of being hustled that makes other tourist locations unpleasant. There are no, or few, cheesy reproductions and dioramas, and no one tries to sell you anything. The villagers, relaxed and chatty, are nevertheless dependent on tourism, and nearly every home in the village is open for meals. And if you happen to miss the last bus back to Beijing, there are plenty of people who are more than happy to put you up.

There is actually very little to do in Cuandixia, but this is part of its charm. Besides wandering the narrow alleyways, inspecting homes and old millstones, you can go for walks in the surrounding hills, which provide excellent views of the village and the environs, particularly the mountain trail on the southern side. The Beijing Hikers (www.beijinghikers.com) organise guides and accommodation to The Great Wall for small groups.

DOUBLE-STONE VILLAGE

As you approach Cuandixia's gate, you pass through a small, run-down village named **Double-Stone Village** (Shuangshitou), also of great age. To some, this may be of more interest than Cuandixia itself – it is of comparable age to its larger neighbour, but for whatever reason, it has escaped the blessing of the tourism bureau. The village, dependent on now-exhausted coal mines, is crumbling. A good number of the courtyard houses are completely abandoned, and the villagers are much older on average. The locals here are not quite as cheerful as Cuandixia's – with good reason – but if you're friendly and considerate, they are happy to take you in and talk with you. They have very long memories.

Above from far left: grey stone courtyard houses of Cuandixia; hills surround Cuandixia; mural in the Double-Stone Village; drying corn.

Food and Drink

The only dining option in Cuandixia is to eat with a local family. Just put your head into a door and ask if the family is making lunch. The food is simple; expect most dishes to cost around 10–15 yuan.

Cuandixia's Preservation

At the end of the Cultural Revolution there were a number of ancient villages scattered around the hills in the Beijing area, but the economic development of the 1980s and 1990s transformed most of them. A story has it that a group of painters from Beijing fell in love with Cuandixia. They talked to the village head, who was amenable to the idea of preservation, and some private money was found in Beijing for repairs. In 1995, Cuandixia became a tourist facility. All reconstruction and repairs are now done according to traditional building methods.

CHENGDE

An overnight stay at the eclectic mountain retreat of Qing emperors.
Explore the manor, its museum and a labyrinth of paths, bridges,
pavilions, halls and temples surrounding several interlocking lakes.

DISTANCE Day 1: is 2.6km
(1.6 miles); Day 2: is 5.3km
(3.29 miles). 250km (150 miles)
east of Beijing; 4 hours by train.
TIME Consider staying for two or
even three days to see everything
in Chengde. It can take a day just
to see the Chengde temples.
START Bishushanzhuang
END Club Peak
POINTS TO NOTE
Daily trains leave from Beijing North,
Beijing East and Beijing Station. The
quickest and most convenient is the
K7711 from Beijing Station departing
at 8.05am and arriving in Chengde at
12.31am. You can return to Beijing by
hourly coaches that leave from the
long distance bus station next to the
railway station. The journey takes
about five hours. In Chengde, walking
from sight to sight is not very practical;
hire a taxi or rent a bicycle for the day.

**A Favourite of
Emperors**
Emperors Jiaqing
and Xianfeng both
died in Chengde, the
latter in 1862, after
which the complex
fell into disuse.

Emperor Kangxi of the Qing dynasty
was drawn to the town of Chengde,
capital of the former province Jehol,
because of its location in a cool, lush
valley with placid lakes and forests,
350m (1,150ft) above sea level. He
ordered the building of the **Mountain
Manor for Escaping the Summer
Heat** (Bishushanzhuang; daily 5.30am–
6.30pm; charge) in 1703, which turned
the previously obscure town into an
imperial resort with a regal garden that
was the largest in China. Remnants of
it can still be viewed today. The manor
was also used in the later years of the
Qing dynasty, when Emperor Qianlong
expanded the residence, incorporating
the styles of China's minorities in his
sprawling retreat as part of an effort to
appease them.

For over a century, emperors and their
retinues enjoyed summer hunting expe-
ditions in Chengde. But after 1820,
when a bolt of lightning killed Emperor
Jiaqing, who was in residence here, the
resort was abandoned. Xianfeng was the
only emperor ever to stay here again,
when he was forced to flee Beijing
during the Second Opium War in 1860.

Around Chengde
If you have just one night in Chengde, spend the first afternoon strolling
through Bishushangzhuang and save
the more strenuous exploration of the
temples for the next morning. In the
Yanshan Mountains that surround the
resort were 12 active temples, varying
in architectural styles. Of the 12, only
eight were in good enough condition to
warrant renovation, and two of those
are still closed to the public. The build-

ings and gardens cover a total area of 560 hectares (1,400 acres) and are surrounded by a wall 10km (6 miles) long.

If you have more time, bizarre rock formations, caves and hot springs await your exploration in the outlying areas. Chengde is quite compact and Bishushangzhuang can be reached easily on foot from the hotels. Public buses and minibuses also run up the main road, Wulie Lu, and stop next to the main gate (Lizhengmen) of Bishushanzhuang.

Little in Chengde is translated for non-Chinese speakers. You may want to hire a guide through the local branch of the **China International Travel Service** (CITS; 11 Zhonghua Lu; tel: 0314-202 6418). Yunshan Hotel *(see p.89 and p.111)* can arrange an English speaking guide for 200 yuan per day, or try haggling with the guides who sell their services at Bishushangzhuang.

MANOR MUSEUM

Start just inside the main gate, at the **Bishushanzhuang Museum ❶** (Bi shushanzhuang Bowuguan; daily 7.30am–5.30pm; charge), which once housed the main palace. Laid out in the traditional linear style of halls and courtyards, it is made of unpainted wood and shaded by tall pines. The exhibits are varied: some rooms display items like Mongolian weapons and dress, others are set up as they were when they were used by the imperial court. Leave by the back door of the museum to get to the park proper. Surrounded by a 10km (6-mile) wall, it is the largest-surviving imperial garden in China.

PAVILIONS AND TEMPLES

On the right, after 100m/yds, begins a maze of paths, bridges, pavilions and halls surrounding several lakes. This area is perfect for strolls, boating and relaxing. Beyond it is the **Literary Nourishment Pavilion ❷** (Wenjinge), one of four imperial libraries. Its central attraction is a rock garden where there is a special place for permanently 'viewing the moon', a trick of light falling on the surrounding rock formations. At the far end of the east side of the park, there is a meadow marked by the pagoda of the **Temple of Eternal Blessing ❸** (Yongyou Sita), which was built by Emperor Qianlong for his

Above from far left: the Mountain Manor for Escaping the Summer Heat is set amid the Yunshan Mountains; lotus pond and lakeside pavilion in Chengde.

mother's 50th birthday.

Heading left from the lake, you come to a more rugged hiking area. Emperors Kangxi and Qianlong designated 72 scenic spots in Bishushanzhuang, but you can find many more yourself. The hills are riddled with small temples and rock formations and topped by pavilion lookout points. A good place to relax and enjoy the greenery is the tea garden at the south-eastern corner of Front Lake, the main lake.

Royal Rebuff

Emperor Qianlong was tremendously fond of the Chengde retreat, and spent a great deal of his reign here. When Lord McCartney and his delegation arrived in Beijing at the end of the 18th century – Great Britain's first official attempt to discuss trading with the Qing government – Qianlong was vacationing in Chengde. Following him there, McCartney was finally granted audience – with an empty throne. On the throne was Qianlong's *Edict on Trade with Great Britain*, stating that Qing-dynasty China had no need of anything that Britain produced. Ministers insisted that McCartney and his retinue kowtow to the empty throne, which they refused to do. Both sides felt the offence deeply, and in the decades following McCartney's visit to Chengde, hostility between the two nations was never suspended for long.

OUTER TEMPLES

Get an early start on your second day and head for the temples beyond the walls of Bishushanzhuang. A good way to do this is to rent a taxi for the morning or day. Hiring a bicycle is also a good idea; you can visit a selection of temples, and the scenery on your ride is excellent. A number of hotels, including Yunshan Hotel, rent out bicycles. The full circuit comprises the **Eight Outer Temples**, but start with these four (below) and see if you hold out.

Little Potala Temple

Little Potala Temple ❹ (Putuo-zongchengzhimiao; daily 8.30am–5pm), which dates from 1767, is the largest and most spectacular complex, modelled on the Potala in Lhasa, Tibet. The beautifully restored halls, staircases and walkways extend over a 22-hectare (54-acre) hillside site. Tibetan-style prayer flags, banners and tapestries hang from the gleaming gold roofs of the temple. The design of the **Temple of Happiness and Longevity** (Xumi-fushoumiao; daily 8am–5.30pm), 1km (¹/₂ mile) east, is based on another Tibetan temple, at Shigatse. At its rear is one of the highlights, an octagonal pagoda that commemorates the 70th birthday of Emperor Qianlong.

Temple of Universal Peace

The **Temple of Universal Peace** ❺ (Puningsi; daily 8.30am–5pm), 3km (2 miles) further north-east and built in 1755, stands out as it is a living monastery with some 50 lamas in resi-

Above from far left:
Temple of Universal
Peace; Tibetan
architecture of
Little Potala Temple;
Temple of Happiness
and Longevity;
Temple of
Universal Joy.

dence. The second hall is laid out with long, low benches for religious study and ceremony. There is an amazing 22m (72ft) carved wooden statue of Guanyin, the Goddess of Mercy, said to be the largest wooden statue in the world. Also known as the Thousand-Arm, Thousand-Eye Guanyin, the statue has 42 arms and an eye on each palm, signifying her power of salvation.

Temple of Universal Joy

Finally, move on to the **Temple of Universal Joy** ❻ (Pulesi; daily 8am–6pm), which lies east of Bishushan-zhuang. This was built in 1766 in honour of Kazhak, Kirghiz and other nobles from north-western China. The complex is similar in style to the main hall of the Temple of Heaven in Beijing. Its main building, the round Pavilion of Morning Light (Xuguangge), sits on a square terrace, symbolising Heaven and Earth, respectively, according to ancient Chinese cosmology. In the pavilion are bronze images of the deities in various acts of passionate embrace and conquest of their enemies – great examples of the wonderful but terrifying imagery in Tibetan Buddhism.

CLUB PEAK

One of the strangest rock formations in the area is at **Club Peak** ❼ (Qing-chuifeng). The legend behind the peak says that it was formed when a monk and a local spirit fought, and the monk's club was turned to stone. At the top of a sloping hill, the stone does look very much like a vast club, bal-anced precariously on its narrow end. You can get there by taking a cable car a few hundred metres north of the Temple of Universal Joy. It is possible to ascend to the platform on which the stone stands, though, of course, it is impossible to mount the stone itself.

Accommodation and Food

There are a few good places to stay in Chengde, such as the four-star **Yunshan Hotel** (2 Banbishan Lu; tel: 0314-205 5588) and **Qiwanglou Hotel** (1 Bifengmen Donglu; tel: 0314-202 4385), a reproduction of a Qing-dynasty mansion. A different option, if you are visiting between March and October, is the **Mongolian Yurt Holiday Village** (tel: 0314-216 3094). Inside the imperial resort grounds, you stay in circular Mongolian yurts. The yurts are air-con-ditioned and have baths and televisions.

Local cuisine centres mainly on wild game, as the area was traditionally reserved as the emperors' hunting ground. Try **Huanggong Yushanfang**, see ❶①, at the Palace Hotel.

Above: the Goddess of Mercy in the Temple of Universal Peace is said to be the largest wooden Buddha statue in the world.

DIRECTORY

A user-friendly alphabetical listing of practical information, plus hand-picked hotels, clearly organised by area, restaurants, listed by type, and bars and nightclubs, to suit all budgets and tastes.

A–Z	92
ACCOMMODATION	106
RESTAURANTS	112
NIGHTLIFE	118
PLACE NAMES IN CHINESE	122

A

AGE RESTRICTIONS

Age restrictions for various venues and activities are lax or non-existent. Laws that ban minors from internet cafés, for example, may exist, but they are rarely enforced. It is also not uncommon to see young children purchasing alcohol or cigarettes, presumably for their parents. At the most, some rides in amusement parks may refuse very small children, and venue ticket prices are often graded according to age.

AIRLINE OFFICES

The majority of foreign airline offices can be found in and around the Yansha Friendship Shopping Mall, on the north-east Dongsanhuan Lu (Third Ring Road). Try www.localnoodles.com for an up-to-date list of addresses and phone numbers.

China's national tourist offices and travel agencies, including hotel travel desks, can give you the current flight schedule of domestic airlines. You can buy tickets from travel agencies or airline booking offices. Travel agencies may be more convenient, and are more likely to have English-speaking staff, although they are likely to charge more. Ticket offices around town sell air tickets, look out for pictures of trains and planes on the signage of small shops. Otherwise, try **China International Travel Services** (CITS; tel: 400 600 8888; www.cits.com.cn)

B

BUDGETING

For many aspects of travel, particularly food and transport, it will be significantly cheaper in China than Western countries. Beijing is trying hard to play catch-up, however, and you may be occasionally surprised by high prices.

Accommodation can cost anywhere from 50 yuan for dormitory beds in youth hostels to luxury prices for rooms in international hotels. An average double room in a hotel will cost from 350 to 600 yuan per night. Dining expenses can likewise vary; in a typical Chinese restaurant you will end up spending 50 to 100 yuan per person. A bus ride is usually 1 yuan and a trip on the subway is 2 yuan, while taxi fares start at 10 yuan and may reach 30 yuan for a longer trip within the city. Admission tickets start from a few yuan for an average park to 60 yuan for the Forbidden City. Most large museums and exhibitions charge 35 to 50 yuan.

BUSINESS HOURS

Business hours vary. Government offices, including banks, are generally open 8am–5pm. Some close earlier and most have a lunch break from noon to 1pm. Offices also open on Saturday mornings, but not on Sundays. The best time to get things done is at the start of the working day – many government offices are reluctant to do anything after 3pm.

Most shops open at 9am and close around 9pm, though if they are still state-run they may close by 6pm. Many department stores and privately run small stores open until 9pm. Money exchange outlets – but not banks – are open seven days a week and also generally operate long hours. At tourist sights, ticket sales may stop 30 minutes before closing time and many museums are closed on Mondays.

C

CHILDREN

Those travelling with children should take care out in the streets, as Beijing's traffic is notoriously chaotic and unpredictable. Illness can be an issue, as well: people from all over China and the world congregate in Beijing, bringing their colds with them, and each season presents its unique health risks. Information and advice on almost every child-related concern imaginable is available on Beijing Kids (www.beijing-kids.com).

CLIMATE

The best time to visit Beijing is from early September through to late November, when it is normally dry and sunny, with moderate temperatures. If you visit between March and May, chances are you will encounter at least one of the annual dust storms that blow in from the Gobi Desert. Summers are hot and muggy, with occasional torrential downpours. The temperature

in the hottest month, July, averages 30ºC (86ºF) but it can occasionally soar to nearly 40ºC (104ºF). Beijing winters are cold and very dry but mostly sunny. The coldest month, January, averages about -5ºC (23ºF), but temperatures can drop to as low as -23ºC (-9ºF). It generally snows once or twice during the winter, and spring may see three or four monsoon-type downpours. Otherwise, there is little precipitation. A polluted haze is the norm for Beijing skies apart from during summer months. During holidays and important events, cloud seeding is often used to help produce glorious weather.

CLOTHING

Shorts, sandals and a sun hat are necessary in summer, while winter calls for heavy coats and warm hats. Locals wear several layers of clothing all winter. One of the best buys in Beijing is silk thermal underwear.

CRIME AND SAFETY

Violent crime is very rare in Beijing, at least when it comes to foreigners. Walking the streets at night is quite safe, and there are no 'bad' parts of town. Women, even those travelling alone, can expect to go unharassed. That said, pickpockets are a danger in most public places. When in crowded areas, keep an eye on wallets and other valuables, and never leave belongings unattended. Scams are the most common risk and the teahouse con

Overcharging and Fake Money
Overcharging in shops and taxis often happens, as does receiving counterfeit bills (usually 100s and 50s, though sometimes 20s as well) as change. In general, it is a good idea to know what things cost ahead of time, and ask that salespeople replace suspect currency.

remains popular around Wangfujing and Tiananmen: friendly locals approach out-of-towners to invite them to a teahouse but don't pick up the extortionate bill. Taxi drivers should always use the meter. The police are willing to receive reports and do what they can to help, but only rarely can they actually retrieve stolen items.

CUSTOMS

Written declarations are required only of visitors carrying more than US$5,000 or who exceed duty-free limits. Chinese customs are especially sensitive to pornographic material as well as publications deemed to be anti-government. Antiques dating from prior to 1795 cannot be legally taken out of the country. Foreigners carrying illicit drugs have been sentenced to long prison terms. Take care when bringing DVDs or CDs out of the country – Chinese customs will let them pass, but customs in your home country may not.

D

DISABLED TRAVELLERS

Beijing is woefully unprepared for disabled travellers: textured paths on the sidewalks, ostensibly for the blind, are the sole concession to the disabled. Wheelchair ramps are very slowly catching on, but they are in so few locations that it makes little difference. Public transport is entirely inaccessible to wheelchairs; even those on crutches will have difficulties.

E

ELECTRICITY

Electrical current runs at 220 volts. Many hotels have 110-volt shaver sockets. Most outlets can accept both parallel- and angled-prong plugs.

EMBASSIES

Embassies are generally located either in the Jianguomen area, Sanlitun or Ritan Park locale.
Australia: 21 Dongzhimenwai Dajie; tel: 5140 4111
Canada: 19 Dongzhimenwai Dajie; tel: 5139 4448
Ireland: 3 Ritan Lu, Jianguomen; tel: 6532 2691
UK: 11 Guanghua Lu, Jianguomenwai; tel: 5192 4000
US: 55 Anjialou Lu, Chaoyang District; tel: 8531 3000

EMERGENCIES

All emergency hotlines provide English-language service.
Ambulance: 120 for service
Fire: 119
Police: 110
Traffic accidents: 122
International SOS: 6590 3419
Beijing tourist complaint hotline: 12301

ETIQUETTE

Chinese society is famous for its complex rules of propriety and etiquette, and it will be difficult for the casual visitor to master them. Luckily most Chinese will make considerable allowances for foreign guests, and a healthy dose of enthusiasm and friendliness will be enough for you to get by. In general, one can never be too modest or appreciative of others' good qualities. Refuse gifts before accepting them (and expect to be refused at first), offer to pay for everything, and try to anticipate others' needs. The 'please-and-thank-you' style of Western courtesy doesn't count for much – you should make an effort to *do* something to express gratitude, even if everyone knows that it is just a show.

Faux pas generally involves embarrassing friends or acquaintances in some way or a lack of necessary flattery. Let mistakes and inconveniences go by, if possible, or if not, bring them up as gently as you can. Avoid putting people on the spot unexpectedly, and, of course, topics of diplomatic sensitivity, such as the sovereignty, Tibet or Taiwan, should be avoided unless someone else brings them up first.

F

FESTIVALS

The three main holidays in China (the three 'Golden Weeks') are Spring Festival (January/February), May First, and October First (China's National Day). Each holiday occasions a week off work, and the entire country more or less grinds to a halt. These are absolutely awful times to travel, as the whole nation tries to take the train all at once, and most businesses close for the week. If you are here for one of these periods, don't plan on getting around much. The government has been considering abolishing the week-long holidays and spreading the days off around the calendar, a move many consider wise and long overdue.

Other important traditional holidays include the Lantern Festival in late February/early March, Tomb Sweeping Day at the beginning of April, and Mid Autumn Day (Moon Festival) in late September/early October.

G

GAY/LESBIAN

Homosexuality is still an awkward subject in China. It was only removed from the list of mental disorders in 2001, and social acceptance has been slow in coming. As Chinese generally dislike public confrontation, homosexuals are rarely harassed openly, but gay pride events are still regularly shut down by the police. The flipside of this is that the underground gay scene is thriving. For English-language nightlife information try www.utopia-asia.com.

GOVERNMENT

Beijing is the capital of the People's Republic of China. Hu Jintao is the general secretary of the Communist Party of China (CPC), president of the country, and the chairman of the CPC-controlled Military Commission. Wen Jiabao is the premier. The 3,000-strong legislative body, the National People's Congress (NPC) meets annually in Beijing. In theory, the NPC can approve or reject legislation, but it is widely regarded as a rubber-stamp parliament. Real power lies with the nine members of the Standing Committee of the CPC Politburo (also known as China's cabinet). Most government bodies have a corresponding body in the party structure, and it is usually the party that wields actual authority. Personal connections and bureaucracy remain key features of day-to-day government and civil service operations.

Beijing is one of the four municipalities with status equal to that of China's provinces, along with Shanghai, Tianjin and Chongqing. It is divided into 12 separate administrative districts. The city's local government set-up mirrors that of the central government; it is led by the Communist Party with limited participation by non-party officials.

The economy is in transition from socialism to a 'socialist market economy'. The capital is still behind many southern and coastal cities in encouraging capitalism. Hence, institutions such as banks and post offices are still caught in the grip of the old system, but the new system is evident in the huge number of privately run restaurants and retail outlets.

HEALTH

Tap water should always be boiled before it is drunk. Some hotels have water purification systems and all sell bottled water and provide flasks of boiled water in guest rooms. Brushing teeth with tap water is not a problem. Bottled water and canned soft drinks are available at tourist sights and sold on most streets.

Although they are not necessarily unsafe, avoid ice cream, yoghurt and drinks from large vats. If buying food from street vendors, make sure it is piping hot and freshly cooked and served in clean dishes, preferably disposable ones. Don't patronise restaurants with dirty utensils or poor food-handling practices, to avoid contracting hepatitis, which is endemic. Wash your hands frequently, and peel or wash fruit. Except in the hotels, most toilets are the crude, though renovated, squat type. Carry your own toilet paper.

Colds and stomach disorders are the most common travellers' complaints. Attention to hygiene goes a long way towards preventing both. Medicines that may come in handy are Panadol, Lomotil (or Imodium), general antibiotics, Pepto-Bismol and aspirin. Watsons, with outlets all over the city, has a wide selection of Western medicines. Malaria prevention medication is not necessary for Beijing or anywhere in northern China.

Consult your doctor or a travel clinic nurse for recommended vaccinations (eg. Hepatitis A) before travelling to China. In the UK, MASTA (Medical Advisory Service for Travellers Abroad) can provide up-to-date information (tel: 0906 8 224 100) on all medical matters.

Medical Services: In case of dire emergency, dial 120 for an ambulance; or call the Beijing International SOS Clinic (5 Sanliton Xiwujie; tel: 6462 9112; 24-hour alarm tel: 6462 9100). Two of the best hospitals for foreigners are the **Sino-Japanese Friendship Hospital** (northern end of Heping Lu; tel: 6422 2952) and the **Peking Union Medical Hospital** (53 Dongdanbei Dajie; emergency tel: 6529 5284). The best place for treatment of serious illness is the private Beijing United Family Heath Centre (B1/F, St Regis Hotel, 21 Jianguomenwai Dajie, Chaoyang District; tel: 8532 1221). All staff speak English.

Pharmacies: These are plentiful and usually open 24 hours. A wide variety of medicines are available, including some that might require a prescription in other countries. Staff often recommend the most expensive products, however, and some suggested remedies might seem positively bizarre to a westerner.

I

INTERNET

Getting online is getting easier and easier in Beijing. Nearly every hotel in Beijing offers some sort of access, either wireless or broadband in the room, or computers in the lobby or business centre. Internet cafés are common and may be less expensive, though some might ask for your passport number before allowing you online. Free wireless internet in cafés and bars is almost ubiquitous.

L

LEFT LUGGAGE/ LOST PROPERTY

Lost property that is presumed stolen should be reported to the Foreigners Section of the **Beijing Public Security Bureau**, tel: 6525 5486. Beijing does not have a central lost-property office, but the **Beijing Tourist Hotline** (tel: 6513 0828) may provide some advice on where to seek help. Taxis are a common place to lose things, which is why it's always advisable to ask for a receipt – this will have the telephone number of the taxi company and your driver's identification number on it. For the airport lost and found, tel: 6459 8333.

M

MEDIA

Newspapers: The English-language *China Daily* reports domestic and foreign news with an official slant. *Global Times* (www.globaltimes.cn) is similar but in a tabloid format. For local listings, pick up a copy of *Time Out Beijing* (www.timeoutbeijing.com) around town. *The International Herald Tribune*, *Asian Wall Street Journal* and international news magazines are available at 5-star hotels, though often a day late.

Television: Most major hotels offer CNN's 24-hour programmes. Star TV from Hong Kong is also available. China Central Television broadcasts

Language
Large hotels usually have many English-speaking staff. Otherwise, you will find that most people speak only a little English. English, French, Japanese, Italian, German and Spanish interpreters can be hired through major hotels or CITS. Prices are negotiable depending on the group's size. For a list of useful phrases and Chinese names of sights, see the pull-out map and p.122–3, respectively.

Maps
A variety of street
and tourist maps
are available free
from the CITS
Information Centre
at 27 Sanlitun Beilu
(tel: 6417 6627).

English-language news and programming on CCTV 9 while local and most imported programmes are broadcast in Chinese. Local radio broadcasts in English and other languages can be heard on 91.5FM and 87.5FM.

MONEY

Currency: The Chinese currency is the renminbi (RMB or 'people's currency') or yuan. Hotel rates are often cited in US dollars, but can be paid in yuan. Foreign currency can be exchanged in banks, the Friendship Store and some big shopping centres. A passport is usually required for any kind of money exchange.

When you change foreign currency into yuan, you get a receipt that allows you to change an equivalent sum of yuan back to foreign currency within six months. Be sure to keep all such receipts.

Chinese money is counted in yuan, jiao and fen. One yuan is 100 fen or 10 jiao; one jiao is 10 fen. Colloquially, a yuan is usually called a kuai and a jiao is called a mao. Bills are denominated in 1, 2 and 5 jiao, and 1, 2, 5, 10, 20, 50 and 100 yuan. There are also 1-yuan, 5-jiao and 1-jiao coins, plus 1-, 2- and 5-fen coins, which are almost worthless.

Credit Cards: Major credit and charge cards like Diner's Club, American Express, MasterCard, Visa and JCB are accepted at all but low-budget hotels. Some restaurants and stores geared toward tourists also accept them.

The most reliable place to cash travellers' cheques is at the Bank of China. Hotels catering to foreigners as well as large branches of other major banks are also able to handle them.

ATMs: Using credit cards to withdraw cash from ATMs is generally practicable, though a bit hit-and-miss. In general, machines marked with Cirrus, Plus, Star, Visa or MasterCard, can be used for withdrawing cash, though there are regular 'network errors'. Outside the airport, the most reliable bank in the city is the Bank of China at the southern end of Wangfujing, followed by the one in the basement of the World Trade Centre. Beyond that, the bigger the bank, the better luck you will have. Always withdraw cash in advance, and never leave yourself dependent on a particular withdrawal succeeding.

Moneychangers: Since Chinese yuan is not fully convertible to foreign currency, there is a small black market for foreign currency.

The main reason why the black market still persists is that it is technically illegal for most Chinese businesses to conduct foreign currency transactions, so they obtain foreign currency through illegal channels. If you do choose to change money on the black market, avoid moneychangers who try to rush you, who ask you to walk into a backstreet with them, or who are not obviously connected with a store. These people are often very good at sleight of hand. The 'safest' places to change money illegally are in the stores and market stalls.

Price Differences: In 1996, China officially abolished the practice of charging foreigners higher prices for hotels, entrance to tourist sights and so on. Most places have complied, resulting in large price rises for Chinese visitors. But vendors at markets, food stands and privately run restaurants often try to charge foreigners more, as in many countries. The best way to deal with this is to find out local prices as soon as possible and insist on paying them, or walk away. If you are unsure of prices in a restaurant, find out the prices of individual dishes before ordering them.

Tipping: In Chairman Mao's time, tipping was thought of as a bourgeois affectation. These days, some hotel staff have come to expect tips, especially restroom attendants and bell boys. Taxi drivers and door attendants do not expect tips. Restaurants catering to foreigners usually add a 10 or 15 percent service charge to the bill, which goes straight to the owners, and waiters will almost never accept tips.

P

PHOTOGRAPHY

Digital and film photography are both relatively convenient in Beijing. Film is readily available, and film development can be done at Kodak chain stores around the city, usually costing 30 yuan or so, plus another 10 or 15 if you want to scan the negatives. Processing for digital photography is also widely available – most photo shops will be able to read memory cards and download photos into discs, or make photographic prints from discs and memory cards.

POSTAL SERVICES

Mail: Hotel desks provide the most convenient service for posting letters and parcels. The International Post Office (tel: 6512 8120; 8am–6.30pm) on Yabao Lu, about 300m/yds north of the Jianguomen junction, handles international mail and is Beijing's poste restante address.

Courier Services: International express courier services in Beijing include DHL (tel: 6466 5566), FedEx (tel: 6468 5566), TNT (tel: 800-810 9868) and UPS (tel: 6530 1234).

PUBLIC HOLIDAYS

The following are official non-working days in China. They may combine with a weekend to provide a longer break.
1 January: New Year's Day
January/February: Spring Festival (a 3-day minimum, dates vary according to the lunar calendar)
8 March: International Women's Day (half-day for women only)
April: Tomb Sweeping Day (1 day, usually April 4 or 5)
1 May: International Workers' Day (5 days)
June: Dragon Boat Festival (1 day, according to lunar calendar)
September: Mid Autumn Festival (1

Above from far left: Chinese bank notes; posing for a picture; bicycles for rent.

day, according to lunar calendar)
1 October: National Day (5 days).

R

RELIGION

For most of the period of Communist rule since 1949, worship of all kinds was discouraged or actively suppressed. Since 1978, the main religions have been allowed to revive, although many urban Chinese are atheists. Buddhism, Taoism, Islam and Christianity are all practised in temples, mosques and churches around Beijing.

Evangelising outside these institutions is forbidden and all religious groups are supposed to register with the government. Even so, Beijing has some underground (i.e. unregistered) Christian groups, particularly Catholic groups loyal to the Pope, which are technically illegal in China.

English language services are held at only a few churches, including the Catholic Nantang Cathedral, 141 Qianmen Dajie (right outside Xuanwumen subway station; tel: 6602 6538), and Protestant Chongwenmen Church, 2 Hougou Hutong, Chongwenmennei (tel: 6513 3549).

S

SMOKING

A nationwide indoor smoking ban at public venues was introduced in 2011 though many, if not most, bars and restaurants are reticent to displease customers by enforcing it. On public transport, smokers will usually stop smoking immediately if asked.

SPORT

All large hotels have sports facilities including gymnasia, tennis courts and swimming pools, which are available to guests at no charge; many also allow non-guests to use these facilities for a fee. There are also a number of private gyms in Beijing, including the international chains **Clark Hatch** (tel: 6466 288) and **Bally Fitness** (Basement Level, Chang An Theatre; tel: 6518 1666), some of which offer daily or weekly rates for non-members.

A number of Olympic venues are open or in the process of being opened to the public for sports activities. The **National Aquatics Centre** (www. water-cube.com), for instance has several swimming pools and a water park. The **National Olympic Sports Centre** (www.bjnosc.com) has a wide range of facilities including tennis and basketball.

T

TELEPHONES

Calls (land line) within Beijing are generally free. In most hotels you can telephone abroad direct, though this is expensive and in some you still need to ask the operator to call for you. In top hotels, you can use credit cards and international telephone cards. China's IDD rates have fallen but are still higher than most Western countries;

remember that costs are halved after 6pm and at weekends.

Payphones which accept phonecards can be found along most city streets and in many hotels and shopping centres. These 'IC' cards (30, 50 or 100 yuan) can be bought at streetside newspaper kiosks or small shops, as well as from hotels. Small shops also sell prepaid internet phonecards called 'IP' cards, which offer considerably lower rates than standard costs and can in theory be used from any phone – before dialling the number you wish to reach, you need to dial a local number printed on the card followed by a PIN number. US credit-phonecard codes from China can be accessed by dialling 108 7901.

The International Post Office on the Second Ring Road north of the Jianguomen intersection (8am–7pm) handles long-distance calls and money orders. The Long Distance Telephone Building at Fuxingmen Dajie (7am–midnight) handles long-distance, conference and pre-booked calls.

Local calls can still be made from roadside booths with attendants, although as cellphones become ever more commonplace, these are disappearing. They generally cost four jiao. These booths can also be used for long-distance calls but charges can be high.

Dial 115 for operator assistance with long-distance calls, and 114 for directory enquiries. The country code for China is 86, and the area code for Beijing is 10, which does not need to be dialled for calls within the city and is not included in the Beijing phone numbers listed in this guidebook.

Fax: Almost all hotels have fax services, although rates vary widely. Expect to pay about 10 yuan per page to send or receive.

TIME DIFFERENCES

Beijing time is eight hours ahead of Greenwich Mean Time (GMT), and there is no daylight-saving time. The entire country follows Beijing's time zone, even at its western extremities.

TOILETS

Public toilets are readily available in Beijing, but that does not mean you are going to like them. Conditions vary wildly, from filthy concrete setups in the *hutong* to plush facilities in larger hotels. New chemical toilets are popping up around town, and while they are a step in the right direction, there is still a long way to go. If you learn no other Chinese characters, you should at least be able to recognise 'man' (男) and 'woman' (女) on the doors.

TOURIST INFORMATION

The **Beijing Tourism Administration** operates a hotline for emergencies and information, tel: 12301. The English spoken at the other end is not always perfect, but if you need help or advice when you are away from your hotel, it is worth a try. Most hotels have their own travel desks for arranging rental cars and organised tours. **China Interna-**

Above from far left: inside the St Joseph's Cathedral; tour group at the Great Wall; alternative signage in the 798 Art District.

tional Travel Services (CITS; tel: 6522 2991; www.cits.com.cn) is the standard national tour agency.

Make good use of the information desk or hotel concierge to check on events and opening and closing times of tourist sights. English language publications listing events are available at most major hotels, restaurants and bars.

TOURS

Hundreds of tour operators eagerly seek out tourist money in a largely unregulated market so pick your tour carefully and bear in mind that many sights in and around Beijing can be reached easily by public transport. The better hotels and hostels will often provide tours to sights such as the Great Wall and Ming Tombs that offer convenience and value for money. For tailor-made tours and translation services try **Bespoke Beijing** (tel: 6528 6603; www.bespoke-beijing.com). **Beijing Xinhua International Tours** offer numerous packages to various sections of the Great Wall as well as theme tours: martial arts, cooking, birdwatching, etc (tel: 6716 0201; www.tour-beijing.com). **China Culture Centre** (tel: 6432 9341; www.chinaculturecenter.org) is a long-standing cultural education agency offering classes, special events and tours of Beijing.

TRANSPORT

Arrival
By Air: The **Beijing Capital International Airport** (Beijing Shoudu Guoji Jichang), 30km (18 miles) from the city centre, connects the city to all parts of China and to the world's major cities. For airport enquiries, call tel: 6454 1100 or visit http://en.bcia.com.cn.

You must check in at least 30 minutes before departure for a domestic flight, though an hour is probably a safer margin, and arriving two hours earlier is wise for international flights. For shorter journeys within China, the train is often a better bet. The airport tax is now included in the ticket price.

The journey between the airport and the city centre takes about 30 to 40 minutes by taxi, but allow an hour or more at busy times. Depending on the destination and category of taxi, the fare will be between 80 and 120 yuan. Beware of drivers who approach you before you reach the taxi rank; ensure the driver uses a meter, or make sure you agree on a price before setting off. The Airport Expressway has an additional 10 yuan toll fare, for which a receipt is provided. If your hotel is near the airport, drivers may be unwilling to take you unless you pay extra – this is illegal, but agreeing to pay will save you much arguing and changing of taxis. The airport express light rail links the airport to Dongzhimen subway station, which gives access to Line 2 and Line 12. The journey takes about 20 minutes, making it quicker than a taxi at rush hours. The service currently runs from Termimal 3 from 6.12am to 10.51pm and from Terminal 2 from 6.35am to 11.10pm.

By Rail: Beijing has three main railway stations: Beijing Railway Station (Beijing Zhan), Beijing West (Beijing Xizhan) and Beijing South (Beijing Nanzhan). Beijing Railway Station and Beijing South are connected to the subway network, with Beijing West set to get it's own station in 2012. Some trains to other parts of China run from the city's three smaller stations. Trans-Siberian trains leave from the Beijing Railway Station for a five-day (via Mongolia) or six-day (via north-eastern China) journey to Moscow. The **Beijing International Hotel** (9 Jianguomennei Dajie; tel: 6512 0507) has an international train ticket booking office. **Monkey Business**, (tel: 6591 6519; www.monkeyshrine.com), a tour agency, specialises in trans-Siberian trips.

If you are arriving on the Trans-Siberian, the same health and customs procedures apply as for international arrivals by air. Taxis are plentiful at the Beijing Railway Station, though there is a long wait. Less expensive, although usually very crowded, are buses that will take you downtown for only 2 yuan.

For travel within China, the best place to buy tickets is the foreigners' booking office to the left of the main concourse inside the Beijing Railway Station, where you can also buy tickets for trains leaving from the Beijing West Station. Beijing West also has a for-eigners' ticket office. Foreigners' ticket windows will often only sell higher-grade seats, however. If you want a sleeper berth, especially in summer or during holidays, buy your ticket at least five days in advance. Return tickets

from major cities are often available, though limited.

By Road: Long-distance buses connect Beijing to many cities. These include Tianjin, Chengde, Beidaihe and Taiyuan. On some routes taking the bus is faster, but generally less com-fortable and less safe than taking the train. The sleeper buses operate longer routes. Beijing's main long-distance bus stations are located at Dongzhimen, Xizhimen and Yongdingmen.

By Sea: The closest seaport to Beijing is neighbouring Tianjin, where ferries depart for Incheon in South Korea, and Osaka, Kobe and Shimonoseki in Japan.

Within Beijing

Taxis: Beijing is oversupplied with taxis, which are inexpensive and con-venient. Prices start at 10 yuan for the first three kilometres, and rise by 2.4 yuan per kilometre thereafter. There is currently a 2 yuan fuel surcharge for journeys over 3km (1.8 miles). Always make sure the meter is switched on before setting off, and ask for a receipt before you get out of the taxi. Drivers usually cannot speak much English. It is a good idea to have your destination and the name and address of your hotel written down in Chinese before setting off. (Hotel name cards in Chinese are very useful for this.) Drivers must post their car number and identity card inside the taxi, so you can note down these details in case of complaints.

Beijing's taxi drivers are generally honest. Do not assume the worst if they take convoluted routes. The city's many one-way streets and complex traffic rules forbid left turns at many junctions. But drivers who line up for hours in front of hotels are often hoping for big fares.

Taxis can also be rented for longer trips, such as whole-day tours or visits to the Great Wall or the Ming Tombs. If you plan to do this, make sure you agree to the total fare and the precise itinerary in advance. Call **Beijing Taxi** (tel: 6837 3399) or simply ask a taxi driver you have come to like.

Bus: Beijing's intricate and ever-changing bus network can be a mystery even to lifelong residents of the city. The English-language website www.bjbus.com can make things easier. Buses are slow and crowded and the distances between stops are sometimes long. On the other hand, buses are a very inexpensive means of transport. A few routes have now been improved, with air-conditioned double-decker buses plying them. Minibuses use the same routes as the buses, and although they offer a faster, more comfortable service at several times the ordinary bus fare, these prices are still low by Western standards. Bus tickets are usually 1 yuan, though they may cost more for long rides or plusher buses.

Subway: Beijing's subway system is fast and very cheap but can be extremely crowded during rush hours and particularly at interchange stations. Currently, all journeys cost 2 yuan and there are trains every few minutes from 5am until 11pm. It is easy to find your way around,

especially as signs and announcements are bilingual. Buy your ticket from the ticket office window or automatic ticket machines. The machines require you to use a touch screen to select your point of departure which can be confusing, but the flat rate of 2 yuan means that selecting any station produces the same result. For convenience, carry coins or 10 yuan notes.

Bicycles: Many hotels have bicycles for hire; if your hotel cannot rent you one, it can advise you where to go. Budget hotels rent out bikes for around 10 yuan per day (excluding the deposit); more upmarket hotels charge in excess of 100 yuan per day or 35 yuan per hour (excluding the deposit). Shops around Houhai also rent single and two-person bikes. Be aware of bike theft, a prevalent form of crime in Beijing.

Pedicabs: If you want to experience travelling through Beijing at a cyclist's pace but don't feel up to cycling yourself, pedicabs – three-wheeled bicycles that accommodate up to two passengers at the back plus the driver in front – can be hired near many tourist sights, especially Houhai and Ritan Park, as well as at larger hotels. Some hotels have their own pedicabs at set prices. Prices are negotiable, from 5 to 30 yuan, depending on the distance you wish to travel and the time of day. Pedicabs are often more expensive than taxis, but as Beijing's rush-hour traffic jams worsen by the day, it can sometimes be faster to walk, cycle or hop into a pedicab than taking a taxi to a nearby destination.

If you are interested in taking a pedicab tour of Beijing's *hutong*, you can arrange this in advance with the **Hutong Pedicab Company** (26 Di'anmennei Xidajie; tel: 6612 3236), or simply head to the Houhai or Dazhalan areas.

Driving
Driving in Beijing is not recommended. Foreign drivers are required to go through a lengthy and costly application procedure to get a local licence (an international licence is a prerequisite). And once on the road you may regret it as traffic rules are often ignored. Companies such as **FESCO** (www.fescochina.com) and **Beijing Expats Service** (www.expatslife.com) have experience helping foreigners obtain driving licences for use in China. It is possible to rent a car and driver for several hundred yuan per day, or a few thousand a month. Try **Hertz** (tel: 800 988 1336; www.hertz.com) or **First Choice Car Rental Service** (tel: 138 1015 6525; www.fcars.cn).

vidual travellers, single-entry visas are valid for entry within three months of issue. Visas are usually issued for 30 to 60 days, and can be extended for another 30 days in China for a small fee at the foreign affairs section of the **Public Security Bureau** (tel: 6404 7799) at Andingmen Dongdajie, just east of the Lama Temple.

Business or study visas are issued on the presentation of a letter or a similar official document from any recognised Chinese organisation. Business travellers can be issued multi-entry visas that are valid for six months to one year.

Carry your passport with you at all times, as it will often be required when you check into hotels, make reservations and change money, as well as for bank transactions. If your passport is lost or stolen, contact your embassy and the Public Security Bureau immediately.

Be sure to leave the country before your visa expires. The fee for over staying runs from a steep 500 yuan per day, up to a maximum 5,000 yuan.

V

VISAS AND PASSPORTS

Valid passports and visas are required of all foreign tourists. Visas may be obtained at embassies or consulates of the People's Republic of China, or through overseas offices of the state-run China International Travel Service (CITS).

Most group tourists are allowed entry through group visas. For indi-

W

WEBSITES

The best places to find information online are probably the websites of local English-language magazines. Those for *That's Beijing* (www.the beijinger.com), listings on *Time Out Beijing* (www.timeoutbeijing.com) and the directory on www.localnoodles. com are the most useful.

Fragrant Hills and Western Suburbs

Fragrant Hill Hotel

Inside Fragrant Hills Park; tel: 6259 1166; fax: 6259 1762; www.xsfd.com; $$

A modern sanctuary in the lush hills north-west of Beijing, beyond the Summer Palace. Designed by the world-renowned architect I.M. Pei, this hotel is one of the more successful meldings of Eastern and Western styles in Beijing. With a swimming pool and Chinese and Western restaurants.

Friendship Hotel

1 Nandajie, Zhongguancun; tel: 6849 8888; www.bjfriendshiphotel.com; $$

Part of a huge, state-run hotel spread out in pleasant grounds close to the Summer Palace and the university district, the hotel has several sections offering a range of prices and facilities. The hotel was built in 1954, and at one time it was the only place in Beijing where foreigners were allowed to live. It is still home to many foreigners working for Chinese state employers.

Presidential Plaza

9 Fuchengmenwai Lu, Xicheng; tel: 5858 5588; www.presidential plazahotelbeijing.cn; $$$

Price for a standard double room for one night:	
$$$$	US$200 and above
$$$	US$150–200
$$	US$100–150
$	US$50–100

A modern addition to the Diaoyutai State Guest House, this has less stringent security and more contemporary facilities, though it still has a definite air of government sponsorship. All 502 rooms have high-speed internet access and multiple phone lines.

Royal Garden Hotel

Shuizha Beilu, Mentougou; tel: 6984 3366/3362; www.lqhotel.com; $$

For atmosphere and facilities, this international hotel, built in classical Chinese style, beats most similarly priced hotels in the city. The only disadvantage is that it is located near the Western Hills, about an hour from the city centre. Its beautiful traditional Chinese garden, though, makes excellent use of the suburban surrounds.

Shangri-La Hotel

29 Zizhuyuan Lu, Haidian; tel: 6841 2211; www.shangri-la.com; $$

This tasteful high-rise hotel has meeting rooms, a ballroom, French and Asian restaurants and many other facilities. On the western edge of the city, it provides a shuttle bus to downtown areas. Chi claims to be the most luxurious spa in Beijing. Shuttle boat services run regularly to the Summer Palace.

Wangfujing and the Foreign Legation Quarter

Beijing Hotel

33 Dongchang'an Jie, Dongcheng; tel: 6513 7766; www.chinabeijing hotel.com.cn; $$$$

Opened in 1917 and recently refurbished, with a long list of famous guests, this is the grande dame of Beijing hotels – its period features give it an air of tradition, in contrast to many newer competitors. It was chosen as the official home of the Olympic Committee for the 2008 Olympic Games. Centrally located, on the corner of Wangfujing Dajie shopping street and five minutes from Tiananmen Square.

Crowne Plaza

48 Wangfujing Dajie, Dengshikou, Dongcheng; tel: 6513 3388; www.crowneplaza.com; $$$$

A fancy hotel that has its own gallery of modern Chinese art and a salon for performances of traditional Chinese music.

Dongjiaominxiang Hotel

23A Dongjiaomin Xiang, Dongcheng; tel: 6524 3311; www.cbw.com/hotel/bj-dongjiaominxiang; $$

This business hotel may not have remarkable rooms, but it does have a great location – in the atmospheric Foreign Legation Quarter, on Dongxiaomin Xiang, two minutes from Tiananmen Square and 10 minutes from Wangfujing Dajie shopping street. The Gold Harbour Seafood restaurant is an excellent spot for Chaozhou and Cantonese fare, and a rooftop Western-style club offers great views.

Fangyuan Hotel

36 Dengshikou Xijie, Dongcheng; tel: 6525 6331; fax: 6513 8549; $

The two-star Fangyuan Hotel may not be particularly smart, but its location just off Wangfujing Dajie and opposite the former home of Lao She, an important

20th-century writer, plus its range of inexpensive rooms, make it worth considering. Breakfast is included.

Grand Hyatt

1 Dongchang'an Jie, Dongcheng; tel: 8518 1234; www.beijing.grand.hyatt.com; $$$$

This first-rate hotel is ensconced in the impressive Oriental Plaza complex. Its enormous concave facade is a landmark of Chang'an Jie. Beijing's premier shopping street, Wangfujing Dajie, is next door and the Forbidden City is just a stroll away. The hotel has an excellent choice of restaurants – Noble Court is one of the better spots in town for Cantonese food, and the Red Moon lounge has a good selection of whiskies.

Haoyuan Hotel

53 Shijia Hutong, Dongsi Nandajie, Dongcheng; tel: 6512 5557; $

Hidden away in a narrow alleyway near the busy Dongdan shopping street, Haoyuan is housed in Qing-era courtyard buildings that feature a traditional combination of brick and red lacquered wood, with curved tiles on the roofs. Rooms, with antique-style furnishings, are clustered around the courtyards, and a small restaurant serves hearty traditional fare at very reasonable prices.

Lee Garden
Service Apartments

18 Jinyu Hutong, Wangfujing Dajie; tel: 6525 8855; www.lgapartment.com; $$$

This is a good option for long-term stays or if you'd like to have a kitchen

Hotel Boom
In recent years, Beijing has experienced a boom in hotel construction, largely due to China's economic progress and in anticipation of the 2008 Olympics. There are few bargains, and this is mainly due to the state-set minimum on room rates.

and other home comforts. The suites range in size from studio to three-room. This 199-room serviced apartment also offers childcare and a children's play area. Some rooms have balconies with a view of the Forbidden City.

Novotel Peace Hotel

3 Jinyu Hutong, Dongcheng; tel: 6512 8833; www.novotel.com; $$

This is a smart and modern four-star hotel with a central location just off Wangfujing Dajie. Its French restaurant, Le Cabernet, is popular for its extensive wine cellar, and often hosts events for Beijing's French community.

The Peninsula

8 Jinyu Hutong, Wangfujing Dajie, Dongcheng; tel: 8516 2888; www.peninsula.com/beijing; $$$$

A modern hotel with Chinese imperial flourishes and tastefully designed rooms. A waterfall cascades down to a lobby full of Chinese antiques, and designer labels fill the shopping arcade. One of the hotel's restaurants, Jing, has drawn notice for its fusion cuisine.

Raffles Beijing Hotel

33 Dongchang'an Jie, Dongcheng; tel: 6526 3388; beijing.raffles.com; $$$$

Occupying the same block as Beijing

Price for a standard double room for one night:	
$$$$	US$200 and above
$$$	US$150–200
$$	US$100–150
$	US$50–100

Hotel *(see p.106)*, this lavish hotel comes with all the luxuries and mod cons expected of the Raffles brand. Its 171 rooms and suites, including some 'personality suites' named after luminaries who had been hosted in them, such as Sun Yat-sen and Henri Cartier-Bresson, blend old-world Oriental elegance with contemporary amenities. Its acclaimed restaurant Jaan serves exquisite modern French cuisine.

Lake District

Beijing Backpackers Hostel

85 Nanluogu Xiang, Dongcheng; tel: 8400 2429; www.backpacking china.com; $

A relatively new hostel located in a *hutong* in Jiaodaokou, right in the middle of the Nanluogu Xiang café and bar scene, and within walking distance of Houhai. This is cleaner and better run than some of the more established hostels in the area, and has also become an information exchange for backpackers travelling to other parts of China. It organises tours to sights such as the Great Wall.

Beijing Bamboo Garden Hotel

24 Xiaoshiqiao Hutong, Jiugulou Dajie; tel: 6403 2229; www.bbgh.com.cn; $

Simple, clean rooms open out to a classical Chinese garden. What it lacks in facilities compared with large, modern hotels, it more than compensates for in atmosphere. Multiple courtyards and its location in a *hutong* offer more peace and quiet than you are likely to find anywhere else in Beijing. The location, close to the

Drum Tower, is slightly inconvenient, but that is part of the charm.

Lusongyuan Hotel

22 Banchang Hutong, Kuanjie, Dongcheng; tel: 6404 0436; www.cbw.com/hotel/lusongyuan; $

This hotel was established in 1980 in the courtyard residence of a former Qing-dynasty official. Stone lions still guard the traditional wooden gate, which leads to the pavilions, trees, rockeries and potted plants that fill the courtyards. The rooms are refined and airy. Great location in a Jiaodaokou *hutong*, and a good breakfast spot even if you are not staying there.

Chaoyang and the CBD

Beijing International Hotel

9 Jianguomennei Dajie, Dongcheng; tel: 6512 6688; www.bih.com.cn; $$

With a good location near the Beijing Railway Station and Henderson and Cofco Plaza shopping centres, this 1,000-room hotel offers a full range of facilities, including a booking office for international flights and trains. The Starlight Revolving Restaurant provides stunning views of the city. This is a popular spot for international conventions.

China World Hotel

1 Jianguomenwai Dajie, Chaoyang East; tel: 6505 2266; www.shangri-la.com; $$$$

Top-class service and accommodation options, with a health club, swimming pool, and shopping and business centres. Its restaurants include Aria, a well-known spot for seafood and wine, and

Scene a Café, good for business lunches. It is well located for business travellers, and provides access to extensive business and conference facilities.

Gloria Plaza Hotel

2 Jianguomen Nandajie, Chaoyang East; tel: 6515 8855; www.gph beijing.com; $$$

Gloria Plaza has a great location on a major junction, opposite the Ancient Observatory and next to one of the main CITS offices. Rooms on the higher floors provide excellent views of the city. There are several restaurants and an American-style sports bar, Sports City Café, which is almost over the top in its homage to basketball.

Hotel G

A7 Gongti Xili, Chaoyang; tel: 6552 3600; www.hotel-g.com.cn; $$

Following the trend for boutique hotels in the capital, Hotel G is an ultra-stylish Workers' Stadium option that is making waves with its attention to detail and service. Includes a Japanese restaurant and popular bar/restaurant.

Jingguang New World Hotel

Hujia Lou, Dongsanhuan Lu (East Third Ring Road), Chaoyang East; tel: 6597 8888; www.jingguang centre.com; $$

A 53-storey building on the eastern Third Ring Road, the Jingguang New World is almost a self-contained town, with its own bakery, restaurants, nightclubs, children's play areas, medical centre and supermarket – and, of course, some of the best views of Beijing.

Above from far left: old-world charm and grand facade of the Raffles Beijing; Oriental chic at the China World Hotel; lush bed and cushions.

Kempinski Hotel Lufthansa Centre

50 Liangmaqiao Lu, Beijing
Lufthansa Centre, Chaoyang
Northeast; tel: 6465 3388;
www.kempinski-beijing.com; $$$

Attached to the Youyi (Friendship) Shopping City, the Kempinski has all the facilities and amenities a discerning traveller requires, including a health club and the pub and restaurant Paulaner Brauhaus, which serves great German beer and cuisine. The hotel is also convenient for access to airline offices and the Women's Street bar district.

Kerry Centre

1 Guanghua Lu (opposite the north
gate of China World Trade Centre),
Chaoyang; tel: 6561 8833;
www.shangri-la.com; $$$$

Aimed at business travellers and linked to a major commercial and shopping complex, the Kerry Centre offers a full range of facilities, from jacuzzis to live-jazz performances, from movie channels to broadband internet access.

Opposite House

11 Sanlitun Lu, Chaoyang;
tel: 6417 6688; www.theopposite-
house.com; $$

This impossibly fashionable Japanese-designed hotel is one of the most stylish spots in town. The lobby seems more like a work of art and the rooms are a minimalist's dream. Two bars and three restaurants are on site.

Red Capital Club Residence

9 Dongsi Liutiao, Dongcheng;
tel: 8403 5308; www.redcapital
club.com.cn; $$$

One of the most exclusive in Beijing, this boutique property is set in a renovated courtyard building that is companion to the Red Capital Club restaurant three *hutong* north. Sip wine in a former bomb shelter beneath the hotel's five suites, each with its own historical theme. Kitschy Communist paraphernalia are scattered around the hotel.

St Regis

21 Jianguomenwai Dajie, Chaoyang
East; tel: 6460 6688; www.stregis.
com/beijing; $$$$

This marvellous and centrally located five-star hotel impresses with an elegant foyer, fine restaurants and a high standard of luxury – the amount of marble in the lobby alone is shocking. Its Press Club Bar is a long-time favourite of the expat business community, while its spa and massage facilities are top-notch.

Traders Hotel

1 Jianguomenwai Dajie, Chaoyang
East; tel: 6505 2277; www.shangri-
la.com; $$$

Well located at the northern end of the China World Trade Centre business complex, the Traders has

Price for a standard double room for one night:	
$$$$	US$200 and above
$$$	US$150–200
$$	US$100–150
$	US$50–100

excellent food, service and accommodation. As it is less expensive than its neighbour, the China World Hotel, the Traders is good for business travellers who are looking for comfort but not top-flight luxury.

Southern Beijing

Kelly's Courtyard
25 Xiaoyuan Hutong, Xidan Beidajie; tel: 6611 8515; www.kellys coutryard.com; $$
This is a small courtyard hotel with rooms that are pleasantly decorated and a nice communal area.

Leo Hostel
52 Dazhilan Xijie; tel: 6303 1595; www.leohostel.com; $
Friendly, bustling hostel on Dazhalan Street offering various tour bookings for travellers, including a popular trip to a 'secret' section of the Great Wall.

Minzu Hotel
51 Fuxingmennei Dajie; tel: 6601 4466; www.minzuhotelbeijing.cn; $$
About 3km (2 miles) west of Tiananmen and popular with long-stay business people. Features a Turkish restaurant.

Great Wall

Commune by the Great Wall
Great Wall Exit at Shuiguan, Badaling Highway; tel: 8118 1888; www.commune.com.cn; $$$$
Twelve spectacular villas – with equally spectacular prices and views – designed by Asia's top architects. Each villa has many bedrooms and a personal butler.

Chengde

Chengde Hotel
19 Nanyingzi Dajie; tel: 0314-590 1888; $$
This is probably the classiest hotel in the area, located right in the heart of town, with easy access to sights and transport, and is as close as Chengde comes to luxury.

Mongolian Yurt Holiday Village
Within the Imperial Resort Grounds Tel: 0314-216 3094; $
Economical and kitschy yurts (containing TVs, washrooms and air-conditioning) are available within the grounds of the imperial resort.

Mountain Villa Hotel
11 Lizhengmen Dajie; tel: 0314-202 3501; $
This good-value hotel is well positioned opposite the imperial resort and has a variety of restaurants.

Qiwanglou Hotel
1 Bifengmon Lu; tel: 0314-202 4385; $$
For its atmosphere alone, this hotel is the best option in Chengde. The small, but exquisite hotel occupies a Qing-dynasty mansion, set just inside the grounds of the imperial resort.

Yunshan Hotel
2 Banbishan Lu; tel: 0314-205 5588; www.cdyunshan.com; $$
This is the main tourist hotel in Chengde, close to the station and with some of the best facilities.

Above from far left: deluxe room at the Kerry Centre; the Kempinski's health club; over-the-top luxury at St Regis; cutting-edge architecture at the Commune by the Great Wall.

Prices and Booking
It is advisable to book in advance during the peak tourist season (June to October). At other times, hotels may offer discounts or special packages; be sure to ask for a discount no matter when you are booking. Most accept reservations from abroad via internet or fax.

Liqun Roast Duck

11 Beixiangfeng, Zhengyi Nanlu,
Qianmen Dongdajie; tel: 6705 5578;
10am–10pm; $$

Once a hidden *hutong* gem, Liqun is now an open secret, but it still serves good Peking duck. Reservations are advised, or you'll need to wait up to an hour, as the converted courtyard home cannot seat too many. Liqun also has a good selection of family-style Chinese dishes; the owners will be happy to sit down with you and discuss your meal.

Alameda

Sanlitun Beijie (inside Nali Mall),
Chaoyang; tel: 6417 8084; daily
noon–3pm, 6–10.30pm; $$

Great *prix-fixé* menus featuring multiple courses of fantastic food with cocktails to match. This routinely wins Beijing's Best Restaurant honour in various competitions, mostly due to the efforts of the chef Vivi Goncalves, who offers a new menu almost every day.

East Ocean Seafood

39 Maizidian Jie, Chaoyang (near
Lufthansa Centre); tel: 6508 3482;
daily 11am–11pm; $$

Price guide for a two-course
meal for one with an
alcoholic drink:

$$$	over 200 yuan
$$	100–200 yuan
$	50–100 yuan

The Cantonese clientele should be your first clue to this restaurant's authenticity and prowess. It is consistently packed, and regularly wins prizes for best Cantonese food in Beijing. It is more expensive than other restaurants, but worth it – the seafood is fresh and the dim sum is great.

The East is Red

266 Baijialou, East Third Ring Road;
tel: 6574 8289; daily 9am–2.30pm,
4–9.30pm; $$

Cultural Revolution-era nostalgia and plenty of kitsch. Watch rousing nightly performances of Communist song and dance and period fare in this truly unique restaurant. It's difficult to find so ask your taxi driver to call for directions.

Guoli Zhuang

500m/yds west of Dongsi Shitiao
Bridge, Dongcheng; tel: 8411 6666;
daily 11am–10pm; $$$

This restaurant is mostly known for its novelty, but what a novelty! Specialising in 'men's health food', it serves a shocking range of animal penises, cooked in a range of styles. You can try grilled deer vitals, cow testicles or a 'three-penis' hot pot if it is variety you're after. Warning: it is quite expensive.

Shunfeng 123

West Gate of the Workers' Stadium;
tel: 6551 3123; daily 10.30am–
10.30pm; $$

Chongqing food is nearly as spicy as the better known Sichuan fare. This restaurant is no exception serving up fiery pork dishes, rabbit hotpot and flavoursome green beans.

Blu Lobster

Shangri-La Hotel, 29 Zizhuyuan Lu; tel: 6841 2211; Tue–Sun 5.30–11pm; $$$

The current menu from Brian McKenna features molecular gastronomy's many implausible wonders. Rumours are a Michelin three-starred chef will take over the restaurant in late 2011, undoubtedly cooking only for those with very deep wallets.

Brasserie Flo

Rainbow Plaza, 16 Dongsanhuan Lu (East Third Ring Road, north of the Changhong Bridge), Chaoyang; tel: 6595 5135; daily 11am–3pm and 6–11pm; $$

Beijing's original French restaurant, and one of the most authentic. This brasserie sticks close to the French essentials and does them right – goose liver with apple, onion soup and imported oysters. And, of course, great French wines by the glass or bottle.

Café Cha

Shangri-La Hotel, 29 Zizhuyuan Lu, Haidian; tel: 6841 2211, ext. 2715; daily 11.30am–2.30pm and 5.30–9.30pm; $$$

Beijing's fusion food craze has produced some questionable artefacts, but the Shangri-La has worked to make sure its experiments stay within the bounds of taste. Though slightly pricey, Café Cha's Asian–Western dishes are excellent, and is particularly well-suited for a Sunday brunch buffet.

Yuelu Shanwu

10 Lotus Lane, Qianhai, Lake District; tel: 6617 2696; daily 11am–11pm; $

Splendid Hunanese food in a sleek setting that combines traditional and modern elements. Its outdoor seating area offers a good view of Qianhai; for privacy, reserve a room upstairs.

Laijinyuxuan Restaurant

Zhongshan Park; tel: 6605 6676; daily 10.30am–7.30pm; $$

Housed in a building resembling a traditional garden house, this restaurant, nearly a century old, serves aristocrat cuisine described in the Qing-dynasty novel *Dream of the Red Mansions*. The *dongcai baozi* (steamed buns with preserved cabbage) is a must-try

Li Family Restaurant (Lijia Cai)

11 Yangfang Hutong, Deshengmennei Dajie, Xicheng; tel: 6613 7509; daily 11am–1.30pm, 5–8.30pm; $$$

Totally unprepossessing, inside and out, this home restaurant serves only four tables of up to 12 seats each day. It is run by Li Shanling, who still has the books and recipes his great-grandfather, an imperial chef, left him. With them, he creates some of the best food

Above from far left: Peking duck; an East-meets-West concoction; hostess at an imperial cuisine restaurant; Café Cha at the Shangri-La.

in the country, hands down. There is no menu – you eat what he makes. World leaders dine here regularly. Book two or three days in advance.

The Taj Pavilion

China World Trade Centre, Chaoyang; tel: 6505 5866, ext. 8116; daily 11.30am–2.30pm and 6–10.30pm; $$

Relaxed Indian restaurant with a large and convincing menu. It may be a tad expensive to eat here, but both the ambience and the dishes are excellent. Go for the lunch buffet – a staple of Indian restaurants in town, but only the Taj Pavilion seems to get it right.

Assaggi

1 Sanlitun Beixiaojie; tel: 8454 4508; daily 11.30am–2.30pm, 6–11.30pm; $$

Italian food served in an elegant setting; the glassed-in rooftop patio is particularly pleasant.

Hatsune

Heqiao Dasha, 8A Guanghua Lu (east of the Kerry Centre), Chaoyang; tel: 6581 3939; 10.30am–2pm, 5.30–10pm; $$

This hip, sleek Japanese joint has a soundtrack and an inventive sushi menu to match. Here, things even Japanese people have never heard of are wrapped in seaweed. But almost everything is delicious. There are three restaurants featuring sushi, barbecue and hot pot.

Saveurs De Coree

29 Nanluogu Xiang, Lake District, Dongcheng; tel: 6401 6083; daily 11am–11pm; $$

This lovely Korean bistro is hidden behind a glass-and-bamboo facade. While most of the city's Korean eateries offer barbecue and little else, you will be able to find more traditional offerings here, from noodles to delicately prepared beef and pork dishes. Try the fixed-price set menu, enjoyed on the rooftop terrace.

Kaorouji

14 Qianhai Dongyan, Lake District; tel: 6404 2554; daily 11am–2pm and 5–11pm; $$

Located in the Shichahai area, this is an old favourite with Beijing's Hui community, opened in 1848. It specialises in lamb, prepared in all manner – grilled, roasted or braised. The caged mynah birds that greet diners in Mandarin are a hit with children. Staff can arrange a meal on a boat on the nearby Qianhai.

Traktirr

5–15 Dongzhimennei Dajie; tel: 8407 8158; daily 10am–10pm; $

Price guide for a two-course meal for one with an alcoholic drink:

$$$	over 200 yuan
$$	100–200 yuan
$	50–100 yuan

Great Russian favourites are served here in a ski-chalet-esque atmosphere. Chicken Kiev is perennially popular, as are various dishes with mushroom and cream sauce, and borscht. If the original location is packed – and it often is – head out to Dongzhimennei Dajie and turn left for its second location.

Shanghainese

Xiao Nan Guo

Third Floor, Building 1, Sanlitun SOHO, 8 Gongti Beilu; tel: 8590 0338; daily 11.30am–9pm; $$

Currently the best restaurant to arrive in the spanking new Sanlitun SOHO development, Xiao Nan Guo is a reputable Shanghai chain serving up specialities such as crab soup dumplings and chicken in Shaoxing wine.

Shanxi

Noodle Loft (Mianku)

20 Dawang Xilu, Chaoyang; tel: 6774 9950; daily 11am–11pm; $$

In this stylishly retro-cool environment with a noodle bar, slurp noodles of every kind and also enjoy other delicious specialities from Shanxi province. Watching the skilled chefs pull, shave, snip and shape noodles by hand before your eyes is almost as fun as eating them.

Sichuan

Fei Teng Yu Xiang

Various locations, including:
36 Xingfu Yicun Sixiang (northern end of the car park opposite the Workers' Stadium), tel: 6417 4988; 1/F, Yehuayue Building, near the south gate of Scitech, tel: 6515

9600; daily 11am–2.30pm and 4.30–10.30pm; $

Chain restaurant featuring *shuizhu yu*, chunks of fish in a huge bowl of peppers and chilli sauce. These restaurants have much more extensive menus than other Sichuan spots and serve an enormous range of specialities that are hard to get elsewhere. The pork ribs, and anything with broccoli, are recommended.

Sichuan Restaurant

14A, Liuyin Jie, Xicheng; tel: 6615 6925/6924; daily 11am–2pm and 5–9pm; $$

Formerly located in a *hutong* behind the Great Hall of the People and frequented by Deng Xiaoping, the late Chinese premier, this well-known restaurant can now be found near Prince Gong's Palace, north of Beihai. The food is still as delicious. Try the Sichuan spicy and sour soup, and diced chicken with hot peppers. Reservations are highly recommended.

South Beauty

Various locations, including:
Pacific Century Place, Gongren Tiyuchang Beilu, tel: 6539 3502; China World Trade Centre, tel: 6505 0809; Oriental Plaza, tel: 8518 6971; Kerry Centre, tel: 8529 9458; daily 11am–11pm; $–$$

This upscale chain is representative of a new emphasis on dining style – the leather sofas and glass installations are just as responsible for its popularity as the Sichuan water-boiled fish and beef cooked on hot stones. It's popular with the business crowd for lunch and dinner.

Above from far left: upmarket restaurant; dough fritters; a chef serving up his creation; *baozi* (steamed buns).

Women's Street
A gourmet zone worth checking out is Nüren Jie (Women's Street), opposite the Israeli embassy, in Chaoyang district. Restaurants here serve Xinjiang, Sichuan, Korean BBQ, Japanese, Malaysian, hot pot cuisines and more. Ignore the touts screaming at you from all ends, pick a spot and dig in.

Three Guizhou Men
Repulse Bay
Second Floor, 8 Gongti Xilu,
Chaoyang; tel: 6551 8517;
11am–11pm; $$
The famous house of numbing spice was recently reopened with a new Sichuan and Hong Kong inspired menu. It's proving a popular spot with the post-club crowd.

Xiheyaju
North-eastern corner of Ritan Park,
Chaoyang; tel: 8561 7643; daily
11am–2.30pm and 5–10pm; $$
Other than Sichuan food, this restaurant, popular with tourists and expats, serves up a range of other regional Chinese cuisines, including Cantonese, Shanghainese and north-eastern. Enjoy your meal in the pretty courtyard.

Southeast Asian

Lau Pa Sak
North-western corner of the intersection of Xindong Lu and Dongzhimenwai Dajie, opposite the Canadian Embassy, Chaoyang; tel: 6417 0952; daily 11am–11pm; $
Southeast Asian noodle, rice and curry dishes, with a smattering of dishes inspired by Singaporean street food. Sambal-flavoured everything is

delicious, as is the dry *beef rendang* curry (good luck finishing it) and seafood stews that smell enchantingly of sea mud. The sweet coffee and curry puffs are must-tries.

Tibetan

Makye Ame
11A Xiushui Nanjie, behind Friendship Store, Chaoyang; tel: 6506 9616; daily 11.30am–2am; $
Authentic food, comfy couches and a cosy atmosphere, until the nightly song-and-dance show, which treads the line between cheese and fascination. Real Tibetan food may consist solely of yak, yak by-products and barley, but Makye Ame has made a brave attempt to turn survival food into a cuisine. Try the goat and yoghurt dishes and yak yak.

Vegetarian

Bodhi-Sake
16 Heiyaochang Jie, Xuanwu; tel: 6355 7348; daily 10am–11pm; $$
Tucked inside the courtyard of a Buddhist temple in southern Beijing, this little eatery is run by its monks. Vegetarian cuisine is served in a tranquil atmosphere marked by chanting and religious music. As in most Buddhist restaurants in Beijing, 'mock meat', made from tofu, nuts and other vegetable proteins, is a main feature. The sausages, beef and fish, are nearly indistinguishable from the real thing.

Gongdelin
158 Qianmen Nandajie, Qianmen; tel: 6702 0867; daily 10.30am–8.30pm; $

> **Price guide for a two-course meal for one with an alcoholic drink:**
>
> | | |
> |---|---|
> | $$$ | over 200 yuan |
> | $$ | 100–200 yuan |
> | $ | 50–100 yuan |

This Buddhist vegetarian restaurant, opened in 1922, is an excellent choice despite the nondescript decor and lacklustre service. Order 'mock meat' dishes, crafted from tofu, mushrooms and vegetables, from its English menu.

Pure Lotus Vegetarian

10 Nongzhan Nanli, Chaoyang Park; tel: 6592 3627; daily 11am–11pm; $$$

Probably the highest-regarded vegetarian restaurant in town, the food may cost the earth but it is certainly heavenly. Tofu, grains and special spices make the fake meat good enough to convert die-hard carnivores.

Vietnamese

Nam Nam

7 Sanlitun Lu, Chaoyang; tel: 6468 6053; daily 10.30am–10.30pm; $

Some of Beijing's best Vietnamese food, served in a very hip French colonial setting. A perfect spot for delicate spring rolls and bowls of noodle soup (though not for big eaters). The good wine list does justice to the French background.

Nuage

22 Qianhai Lake East Bank; tel: 6401 9581; daily 11am–1pm; $$

This Vietnamese restaurant's languid style and lakeside location give it the sultry atmosphere of a tropical escape.

Xinjiang

Afanti

2 Houguaibang Hutong, Chaoyangmennei Dajie, Dongcheng; tel: 6525

1071; daily 11am–midnight; $$

Lively restaurant serving sumptuous roast lamb, kebabs and flatbreads. Live music and dancing usually inspire patrons to jump atop their tables to join in the fun. Reservations are advised.

Xinjiang Red Rose

7 Xingfu Yicun, opposite the Workers' Stadium North Gate; tel: 6415 5741; daily 11am–11pm; $$

Hookah pipes, nightly music, Uighur dancing girls and excellent *dapaiji* ('big plate chicken'). Large groups can get rather boisterous.

Yunnanese

Dali Courtyard

67 Xiaojingchang Hutong, Gulou Dongdajie; tel: 8404 1430; daily 11am–2pm, 6–11pm; $$

Set in a beautiful courtyard, this popular restaurant offers a set menu only according to what the chefs are prepared to cook on a given day.

Golden Peacock

16 Minzu Daxue Beilu, Weigongcun, Haidian; tel: 6893 2030; daily 11am–9pm; $

Ethnic minority cuisine is often most authentic in the vicinity of the Central University for Nationalities, and the Golden Peacock, serving the food of the Dai minority, is exceptional. The waitstaff are all from Yunnan, as are the regional delicacies such as fried potato balls, sticky rice in half a pineapple, and fish done fifty different ways.

Chaoyang and CBD

Blue Frog

Third floor, Building 4, Sanlitun Village; tel: 6417 4030

Though more famous for its hamburgers, Blue Frog is also a place Sanlitun Village's shoppers are grateful for thanks to its quality liquid refreshments. The rooftop and well-trained staff are a bonus.

Centro

Lobby, Kerry Centre, 1 Guanghua Lu; tel: 6561 8833/42;

The Kerry Centre aimed to make Centro the poshest lounge in town, and to a large extent it has succeeded. From the decor to the performing bartenders, everything about Centro could easily stray over the top, but as a whole it still manages to stay classy. Jazz acts imported from the US play nightly, international businessmen relax after a day of deal-making, and London-priced cocktails are half-price before 6pm.

Destination

Opposite Workers' Stadium West Gate; tel: 6551 5138

By far the city's largest dedicated gay bar with a clientele that is 90 percent male. Destination is a popular spot for dancing and cruising that sometimes hosts community events.

Drei Kronen 1308

5 China View, Workers' Stadium East Road; tel: 6503 5555

A counterintuitively large microbrewery serving wallet-lightening but excellent steins of pilsner, wheat beer and dark beer. Staff manage to be friendly despite being decked out in clichéd German costume: think lederhosen or braided pigtails.

Face Bar

Just south of Workers' Stadium South Gate; tel: 6551 6788

A tasteful Asian cocktail lounge with thoughtful bartenders and red-baize pool table. Expect a service charge on top of the already costly price of drinks. Bar snacks such as excellent samosas can be brought in from the adjoining Thai and Indian restaurants.

First Floor

Sanlitun Houjie; tel: 6413 0587

The small bar street running parallel to Sanlitun Lu has become rather seedy in recent years but First Floor is a very decent pub serving quality brews such as Guinness and very acceptable food. The crowd is mostly made up of regulars.

Fubar

Inside Workers' Stadium East Gate; tel: 6593 8227

A speakeasy themed bar tucked away behind a hidden door at the back of a hot dog stall may sound like a gimmick too far but the experienced bar manager is something of a local celebrity and has worked hard to make this a word-of-mouth success. Rarely seen bottles such as Maker's Mark and Green Chartreuse sit proudly behind the bar.

LAN Club

4/F LG Twin Towers, B12 Jianguomenwai Dajie; tel 5109 6012

A glamorous, Philippe Starck-designed interior makes this one of Beijing's most eye-catching venues. LAN Club boasts an impressive wine cellar and cigar lounge but also courts the younger crowd with themed parties.

Paddy O'Sheas

28 Dongzhimenwai Dajie, Sanlitun; tel: 6415 6389

An Irish pub popular for draught Guinness, reasonably priced drinks and standard bar food. Televised sports matches and pool/darts upstairs make this a popular spot for sports fans.

Punk

The Opposite House, Sanlitun Lu; tel: 6410 5222

Located in the basement of boutique hotel The Opposite House, Punk seems effortlessly trendy though the management put a lot of work into getting things right. Expect great cocktails and skilled DJs on weekends.

The Tree

43 Sanlitun Reijie, behind Poachers Inn; tel: 6415 1954

Tucked round the corner away from Sanlitun's less sophisticated bars, the Tree's cosy pub atmosphere makes it a perennial favourite. Belgium beers and an authentic pizza oven ensure this is one of Sanlitun's best spots for lunch or an evening's entertainment.

Vics

Inside Workers' Stadium North Gate; tel: 5293 0333

Vics is the largest nightclub in the Workers' Stadium north gate section and for all its faults keeps the crowds happy and remains popular year after year. Expect crowds of fashionable young people and loud hip-hop music.

Xiu

Sixth Floor, Park Life (opposite Park Hyatt lobby), 2 Jianguomenwai; tel: 8567 1108

The sixth floor of part of the Park Hyatt complex, this bar club attracts a mixed response. Its interior - encompassing a terrace, saloon and several rooms – and fantastic views will impress though some customers complain of high drink prices and service problems.

Chaoyang Park

Goose 'n' Duck Pub

Green Lake International Tower; tel: 5928 3045

Flat-screen TVs and video games make this a rough 'n' ready spot for a lager or two but it draws a loyal, regular crowd and is a good place to meet up with expats.

Mokihi

Third Floor, C12 Haoyun Jie; tel: 5867 0244

A Japanese cocktail bar (next to Edomae Sushi, look out for the sign) that justifies high prices with precision-made cocktails including the implausible wasabi martini and wonderful Earl Grey MarTEAni. A classic-styled bar and jazz music make this a hard place to leave.

The World of Suzie Wong

1A Nongzhanguan Lu; tel: 6500 3377

This three-floored opium-den styled nightclub is responsible for kick-starting the whole Chaoyang Park-area nightlife scene. The occasional celebrity visitor and a female clientele who clearly put more effort into looking glamorous than enjoying their drinks will make this Beijing mainstay too pretentious for some.

Lake District

Aluss

Second Floor, 141 Dongcheng; tel: 8400 2628

A simple *hutong* bar serving a fine selection of imported beers. The owner puts his own photography up on display as well as other local artworks.

Café Heaven and Earth

2 Qianhai Beiyan; tel: 6657 1870

This café stocks a variety of herbal teas as well as coffee, beer and cocktails. There is also a small Japanese restaurant attached. Wi-fi available.

Drum and Bell Cafe

41 Zhonglouwan Hutong; tel: 8403 3600

One of the best spots for coffee, or even beer, on a roof garden overlooking a public area between the ancient Drum and Bell towers where locals practice tai chi, spin diabolos and gossip.

El Nido

59 Fangjia Hutong; tel: 8402 9495

Fangjia Hutong is styling itself as a smaller version of the 798 Art District.

Though its artistic and theatrical ambitions have yet to be fully realised, the area has become a successful, though small, bar and restaurant area. El Nido attracts a Bohemian crowd with obligatory absinthe and French wines.

ING

55a Wudaoying Hutong; tel: 6401 7769

A hutong bar and café that strives to carve a niche out for itself on trendy Wudaoying Hutong. It has a loft, comfy couches downstairs, goldfish and even two iguanas.

MAO Livehouse

111 Gulou Dongdajie; tel: 6402 5080; www.maolive.com

This no-nonsense rock club has become a mainstay of Beijing's music scene. Cheap drinks and loud music attract a young crowd. The venue occasionally falls foul of fire safety regulations and closes for a time.

No Name Bar

3 Qianhai Dongyan, Houhai; tel: 6401 8541

A tasteful interior of bamboo and tropical plants, plus the lakes views, make this one of Houhai's best bars or potential coffee stop. Somehow, perhaps the management's unwillingness to even chose a name for their venue, the crowds have yet to discover this Houhai watering hole.

Siif

67 Beiluoguxiang, Dongcheng; tel: 6406 9496

Above: Lotus Lane
Bar Strip.

The long, bustling *hutong* Nanluogu Xiang can hardly be considered off the beaten path any longer. Hidden in nearby Beiluoguxiang, Siif is definitely worth hunting out for cheap drinks and a relaxed crowd. There's a simple balcony and even simpler basement dance floor.

Tao Yao Bar

Beiguanfang Hutong, (300m/yds west of Silver Ingot Bridge); tel: 8322 8585

This Tibetan-themed bar carves itself a nice little niche out of the area's mish-mash of nightlife. Milk tea, of course, and beers are served up just far enough away from the throngs of Houhai tourists to create a peaceful spot.

Yugong Yishan

3 Zhangxizhong Lu, Dongcheng; tel: 6404 2711

Yugong Yishan is by far Beijing's best-known live music venue. Their sound system is decent and the man-agement just professional enough to regularly attract foreign talent.

Grungy locals grudgingly stump up full prices for drinks and the occa-sional pop or rock star can be seen at the bar.

Western Suburbs

The Garden Bar and Terrace

Shangri-La Hotel, 29 Zizhuyuan Lu; tel: 6841 2211

The ideal spot for drinks after a visit to the Summer Palace, this wine bar's garden impresses with a marble bridge over a tree-shaded stream, lazy Koi carp and a decent selection of wine at reasonable prices.

Central Beijing

Yin Bar

33 Qihelou Dajie, (rooftop of the Emperor Hotel), Dongcheng; tel: 6523 6877

With views that most bars can only dream of (taking in the Forbidden City, Jingshan Park and Tiananmen Square), Yin Bar has little shame in charging high prices for drinks but has generously included a jacuzzi on it's wooden-terraced roof.

Left: Suzie Wong Bar.

PLACE NAMES IN CHINESE

English	Hanyu Pinyin	Chinese
798 Art District	798 Yìshùqū	798艺术区
Ancient Observatory	Gǔ Guānxiàngtái	古观象台
Beihai Park	Běihǎi Gōngyuán	北海公园
Beijing Botanical Gardens	Běijīng Zhíwùyuán	北京植物园
Bell Tower	Zhōnglóu	钟楼
Blue Zoo	Fùguó Hǎidǐ Shìjiè	富国海底世界
Caochangdi	Cǎochǎngdì	草场地
Changling	Chánglíng	长陵
Chengde	Chéng Dé	承德
Chi'enmen 23	Qiánmén èrshísān hào	前门23号
China World Trade Centre	Zhōngguó Guójì Màoyì Zhōngxīn	中国国际贸易中心
Chinese Ethnic Culture Park	Zhōngguó Mínzúyuán	中国民族园
Coal Hill (Jingshan) Park	Jǐngshān Gōngyuán	景山公园
Confucius Temple	Kǒng Miào	孔庙
Cuandixia	Cuāndǐxià	爨底下
Daguanlou Cinema	Dàguānlóu	大观楼
Dashanzi	Dàshānzi	大山子
Dazhalan Street	Dàzhálán Jiē	大栅栏街
Dingling	Dìnglíng	定陵
Ditan Park	Dìtán Gōngyuán	地坛公园
Donghuamen Night Market	Dōnghuámén Yèshìchǎng	东华门夜市场
Dongsi Shitiao	Dōngsì Shítiáo	东四十条
Double-Stone Village	Shuāngshítóu	双石头
Drum Tower	Gǔlóu	鼓楼
Forbidden City	Gùgōng/Zǐjìnchéng	故宫/紫禁城
Foreign Legation Quarter	Dōngjiāomín Xiàng	东交民巷
Fragrant Hills Park	Xiāngshān Gōngyuán	香山公园
FunDazzle	Fāndǒulè	翻斗乐
Great Hall of the People	Rénmín Dàhuìtáng	人民大会堂
Great Wall	Wànlǐ Cháng Chéng	万里长城
Guanghua Buddhist Temple	Guǎnghuà Sì	广化寺
Hongqiao Market	Hóngqiáo Shìchǎng	红桥市场
Houhai (Rear Lake)	Hòu Hǎi	后海
Huanghuacheng	Huánghuāchéng	黄花城
Imperial Academy	Guózǐjiàn	国子监
Imperial City Art Gallery	Huángchéng Yìshùguǎn	皇城艺术馆
Jianwai SOHO	Jiànwài SOHO	建外SOHO
Lama Temple	Yōnghégōng	雍和宫
Little Potala Temple	Pǔtuǒzōngchéngzhīmiào	普陀宗乘之庙
Liulichang Street	Liúlíchǎng Jiē	琉璃厂街
Mao Zedong Mausoleum	Máo Zhǔxí Jìniàntáng	毛主席纪念堂

Ming Tombs	Shísānlíng	十三陵
Monument to the People's Heroes	Rénmín Yīngxióng Jìniàn Bēi	人民英雄 纪念碑
Mountain Manor for Escaping the Summer Heat	Bìshǔshānzhuāng	避暑山庄
Mutianyu	Mùtiányù	慕田峪
Nanluogu Xiang	Nánluógǔ Xiàng	南罗鼓巷
Nanxincang	Nánxīncāng	南新仓
National Aquatics Centre	Guójiā Yóuyǒng Zhōngxīn	国家游泳中心
National Centre for the Performing Arts	Guójiā Dàjùyuàn	国家大剧院
National Stadium	Guójiā Tǐyùchǎng	国家体育场
Natural History Museum	Zìrán Bówùguǎn	自然博物馆
Old Summer Palace	Yuánmíngyuán	圆明园
Olympic Park	Àolínpǐkè Gōngyuán	奥林匹克公园
Ox Street Mosque	Niújiē Qīngzhēnsì	牛街清真寺
Palace of Prince Gong	Gōng Wángfǔ	恭王府
Poly Plaza	Bǎolì Dàshà	宝利大厦
Poly Plaza Museum	Bǎolì Yìshù Bówùguǎn	宝利艺术博物馆
Qianhai (Front Lake)	Qiánhǎi	前海
Qianmen (Front Gate)	Qiánmén	前门
Ritan Park	Rìtán Gōngyuán	日坛公园
St Joseph's Cathedral	Dōngtáng	东堂
St Michael's Church	Shèngmǐ'è'ěr Táng	圣米厄尔堂
Sanlitun	Sānlǐtún	三里屯
Silk Market	Xiùshuǐ Shìchǎng	秀水市场
Simatai	Sīmǎtái	司马台
Summer Palace	Yíhéyuán	颐和园
Temple of the Azure Clouds	Bìyúnsì	碧云寺
Temple of Heaven	Tiāntán	天坛
Temple of the Source of Buddhist Doctrine	Fǎyuánsì	法源寺
Tiananmen Gate	Tiānānmén	天安门
Tiananmen Square	Tiānānmén Guǎngchǎng	天安门广场
Tucheng Park	Tǔchéng Gōngyuán	土城公园
Wangfujing Street	Wángfǔjīng Dàjiē	王府井大街
Women's Street	Nǚrén Jiē	女人街
Workers' Stadium	Gōngrén Tǐyùchǎng	工人体育场
Wudaokou	Wǔdàokǒu	五道口
Wudaoying Hutong	Wǔdàoyíng Hú tòng	五道营
Xianyukou Food Street	Xiānyúkǒu	鲜鱼口
Yaxiu Market	Yǎxiù Shìchǎng	雅秀市场
Zhaoling	Zhāolíng	昭陵
Zhongshan Park	Zhōngshān Gōngyuán	中山公园
Zongbu Hutong	Zǒngbù Hútóng	总部胡同

Above from far left: ducks on Houhai Lake; practising calligraphy in Beihai Park; Chinese teapots; *hutong* scene.

Useful Phrases
For more useful phrases, see the pull-out map.

CREDITS

Insight Step by Step Beijing
Written by: Eric Abrahamsen
Updated by: David Drakeford
Commissioned by: Tom Le Bas
Proofread and indexed by: Catherine Jackson
Edited by: Pamela Afram
Series Editor: Carine Tracanelli
Map Production: APA Cartography Department
Picture Manager: Steve Lawrence
Art Editor: Ian Spick
Production: Tynan Dean and Linton Donaldson
Photography by: Apa: Ming Tang-Evans, Richard Nowitz and Lee Hin Mun, except: Alamy 92B; China World Hotel 113TL; Corbis 20T, 20MB, 21T, 21MT, 21MC, 21MB, 21B, 55M, 93TR; Grand Hyatt 111TL, 111TR; Imagine China 6CL, 36B, 54TL, 62T, 69B, 75TL, 80B, 83TR, 88TL, 88TR, 89TL, 89TR, 89MT, 89MB, 90TL, 90TR, 90MT, 90MB, 91T, 92TL, 92TR, 93TL, 93M, 99T, 100T; istockphoto 2/3; Kempinski Hotels 114TR, 115TR; Kerry Centre 114TL; Raffles Beijing Hotel 112TR; Shangri-La Hotel 110T, 117TR; Topfoto 20MT

Front Cover: istockphoto (top and bottom right); Ming Tang-Evans/Apa (bottom left)

Printed by: CTPS-China

DISTRIBUTION

Worldwide
APA Publications GmbH & Co. Verlag KG (Singapore branch)
7030 Ang Mo Kio Ave 5
08-65 Northstar @ AMK, Singapore 569880
Email: apasin@singnet.com.sg

UK and Ireland
Dorling Kindersley Ltd (a Penguin Company)
80 Strand, London, WC2R 0RL, UK
Email: sales@uk.dk.com

US
Ingram Publisher Services
One Ingram Blvd, PO Box 3006
La Vergne, TN 37086-1986
Email: customer.service@ingrampublisher services.com

Australia
Universal Publishers
PO Box 307
St. Leonards NSW 1590
Email: sales@universalpublishers.com.au

CONTACTING THE EDITORS

We would appreciate it if readers would alert us to errors or outdated information by writing to us at insight@apaguide.co.uk or Apa Publications, PO Box 7910, London SE1 1WE, UK.

www.insightguides.com

THE WORLD OF
INSIGHT GUIDES

Different people need different kinds of travel information. Some want background facts. Others seek personal recommendations. With a variety of different products – Insight Guides, Insight City Guides, Step by Step Guides, Smart Guides, Insight Fleximaps and our new Great Breaks series – we offer readers the perfect choice.

Insight Guides will turn your visit into an experience.

INDEX

798 Art District **72–3**

A

accommodation **106–11**
acrobatics **18–9**
age restrictions **92**
airline offices **92**
Altar of Heaven
(Temple of Heaven) **49**
Ancient Observatory **66**
art galleries **51, 71–4**
Avenue of Stone Figures
(Ming Tombs) **79**

B

bars and clubs **18, 118–21**
Beihai Park
(North Lake Park) **46–7**
Beijing Antique City **16**
Beijing Botanical Gardens **77**
Beijing Zoo **61**
Belgian Legation, former
35–6
Bell Tower **42**
Bishushanzhuang Museum
(Chengde) **87**
Blue Zoo **61**
Boxer Rebellion **20, 33–34, 58**
Bridge of Seventeen Arches
(Summer Palace) **60**
British Legation, former **37**
budgeting **92**
Building for Reading Old
Inscriptions (Jade Island,
Beihai Park) **47**
business hours **92**

C

Caochangdi **73–4**
Central Business
District **64–5**
Changling (Ming Tombs)
80–1

Changping **78–9**
Chengde **86–9**
children **93, 61–3**
China Central Television
Station Tower (CCTV) **65**
Chinese Ethnic
Culture Park **69–70**
city overview **10–3**
Cixi, empress dowager **20,
58–60**
climate **93**
clothing **93**
Club Peak (Chengde) **89**
Coal Hill (Jingshan) Park **31**
Confucius Temple **39–40**
crime and safety **93–4**
Cuandixia **84–5**
Cultural Revolution **21**
customs **94**

D

Daguanlou Cinema **55–6**
Dashanzi **71–3**
Dazhalan **54–7**
Deng Xiaoping **21**
Diamond Throne Pagoda
(Fragrant Hills Park) **75**
Dingling (Ming Tombs) **80**
directory **92–125**
disabled travellers **94**
Ditan Park **41**
Donghuamen Night
Market **53**
Dongsi Shitiao **67**
Double-Stone Village **85**
Dragon King's Temple
(Summer Palace) **60**
Drum Tower **42**
Dutch Legation, former **37**

E

Echo Wall
(Temple of Heaven) **49**
electricity **94**

embassies **94**
emergencies **94**
etiquette **94–5**

F

festivals **41–2, 95, 99**
Five Dragon Pavilion
(Beihai Park) **46**
food and drink **14–5, 112–17**
Forbidden City (Imperial
Palace/Palace Museum)
10, 20, 28–31, 51
Foreign Legation
Quarter **33–7**
Fragrant Hills Hotel
(Fragrant Hills Park) **77**
Fragrant Hills Park **75–7**
Fragrant Hills Temple
(Fragrant Hills Park) **77**
French Barracks, former **35**
French Legation, former **35**
French Post Office, former **35**
FunDazzle **61**

G

Gate of Divine Warrior
(Forbidden City) **31**
Gate of Heavenly Purity
(Forbidden City) **31**
gay and lesbian travellers **95**
government **95–6**
Great Hall of the People
(Renmin Dahuitang) **26–7**
Great Palace Gate
(Ming Tombs) **79**
Great Wall **20, 81–3**
Guanghua Buddhist Temple
44

H

Hall of 500 Luohan
(Fragrant Hills Park) **76**
Hall of Abstinence

(Temple of Heaven) **49**
Hall of Benevolence
and Longevity
(Summer Palace) **60**
Hall of Dispelling Clouds
(Summer Palace) **59**
Hall of Eminent Favours
(Ming Tombs) **81**
Hall of Great Achievement
(Confucius Temple) **40**
Hall of Jade Ripples
(Summer Palace) **60**
Hall of Laughter
(Summer Palace) **60**
Hall of Middle Harmony
(Forbidden City) **30**
Hall of Prayer for Good
Harvests (Temple of
Heaven) **48, 49**
Hall of Preserving Harmony
(Forbidden City) **30**
Hall of Ripples (Jade Island,
Beihai Park) **46**
Hall of Supreme Harmony
(Forbidden City) **30**
Hall of Universal Peace (Jade
Island, Beihai Park) **47**
Hall of Virtuous Light
(Summer Palace) **59**
health **96–7**
Hill of Longevity
(Summer Palace) **59**
history **20–1**
Hongqiao Market **16, 50**
Houhai (Rear Lake) **43–4**
Huanghuacheng
(Great Wall) **83**
Huangshicheng **51**
Hu Jintao **21, 95**
Hungarian Legation,
former **34–5**

Imperial Academy **40**
Imperial City Art Gallery **51**
Imperial Vault of Heaven
(Temple of Heaven) **49**

Incense Burner Peak
(Fragrant Hills Park) **76–7**
Inner Court
(Forbidden City) **29**
internet **97**
Italian Legation, former **34**

J

Jade Island (Beihai Park) **46**
Japanese Legation, former **37**
Jiang Zemin **21**
Jianlou (Arrow Tower) **25**
Jianwai SOHO **65**

K

Kunming Lake
(Summer Palace) **60**

L

Lake District **42–7**
Lama Temple **38**
left luggage/lost property **97**
Literary Nourishment Pavilion
(Chengde) **87**
Little Potala Temple
(Chengde) **88**
Liulichang **56**
Long Corridor
(Summer Palace) **60**
Long Corridor
(Temple of Heaven) **49**
Lotus Lane (Qianhai) **45**

M

Mao Zedong **21, 27, 28**
Mao Zedong Mausoleum **26**
maps **98**
Marble Boat
(Summer Palace) **60**
Marco Polo **20**
media **97–8**
Meridian Gate
(Forbidden City) **30, 52**
Ming Tombs **79–81**

Miniature Western Heaven
(Beihai Park) **46**
money **98–9**
Monument to the People's
Heroes **26**
Mountain Manor for
Escaping the Summer Heat
(Bishushanzhuang,
Chengde) **86**
Mutianyu (Great Wall) **81–3**

N

Nanluogu Xiang **43, 44**
Nanxincang **67–8**
National Aquatics Centre **70**
National Centre of Performing
Arts (National Grand
Theatre) **19, 26**
National Museum of China
25, 27
National Stadium **70**
Natural History Museum **50**
nightlife **18–9, 118–21**
Nine Dragon Screen
(Beihai Park) **46**
Nine Dragon Screen
(Forbidden City) **31**

O

Olympic Games **21, 69–70**
Olympic Park **70**
Opium Wars **20, 26, 42, 48**
Oriental Plaza **17, 32**
orientation **10–21**
Outer Court
(Forbidden City) **29**
Ox Street Mosque **57**

P

Pagoda of Buddhist Virtue
(Summer Palace) **59**
Palace of Heavenly Purity
(Forbidden City) **31**
Palace of Peace and Longevity
(Forbidden City) **31**

Palace of Prince Gong **45**
Panjiayuan Market **16**
Pan Shiyi **65**
Pavilion of Precious Clouds
    (Summer Palace) **59**
Pavilion of Shared Coolness
    (Jade Island,
    Beihai Park) **46**
Pavilion of Ten Thousand
    Happinesses
    (Lama Temple) **39**
Peking Club, former **35**
Peking duck **15, 27, 68, 112**
Peking opera **18, 41, 56**
Peony Garden **41**
photography **99**
Plate for Gathering Dew
    (Jade Island, Beihai Park)
    46
Police Museum **37**
Poly Museum **68**
Poly Plaza, New **68**
Poly Plaza, Old **68**
postal services **99**
public holidays **99–100**

Q

Qianhai (Front Lake) **45**
Qianmen (Front Gate) **24**

R

religion **100**
Residence of Liang Sicheng,
    former **66**
Residence of Song Qingling,
    former **44**
restaurants **112–17**
Ritan Park **62–3**
Round Town (Beihai Park) **47**
Russian Legation, former
    36–7

S

Sackler Gallery **60**
Sanlitun **53**

shopping **16–7**
Silk (Xiushui) Market **16, 65**
Silver Ingot Bridge
    (Houhai) **44**
Simatai (Great Wall) **83**
Sino-Japanese War **20, 33**
smoking **100**
Spanish Legation, former **36**
Spectacles Lake
    (Fragrant Hills Park) **76**
Spirit Way (Ming Tombs) **79**
sport **100**
St Joseph's Cathedral **33, 53**
St Michael's Church **35**
Sumeru Temple
    (Summer Palace) **59**
Summer Palace
    (Yiheyuan) **58–60**
Summer Palace, old
    (Yuanmingyuan) **59, 68**
Sun Yat-sen **20, 28, 44, 75**
Sun Yat-sen Memorial Hall
    (Fragrant Hills Park) **75**

T

telephones **100–01**
Temple of the Azure Clouds
    (Fragrant Hills Park) **75–6**
Temple of Clarity
    (Fragrant Hills Park) **76**
Temple of Eternal Blessing
    (Chengde) **87**
Temple of Eternal Peace
    (Jade Island, Beihai
    Park) **47**
Temple of Happiness and
    Longevity (Chengde) **88**
Temple of Heaven **48–50**
Temple of the Sea of Wisdom
    (Summer Palace) **59**
Temple of the Source of
    Buddhist Doctrine **56–7**
Temple of Universal
    Joy (Chengde) **89**
Temple of Universal
    Peace (Chengde) **88**

Three Echo Stones
    (Temple of Heaven) **49**
Tiananmen Gate **28**
Tiananmen Square **21, 27,
    51–2**
time differences **101**
toilets **101**
tourist information **101–02**
tours **102**
transport **102–05**
Tucheng Park **69**

V/W

visas and passports **105**
Wangfujing **32–3, 53**
Wangfujing Foreign
    Languages Bookstore **32–3**
websites **105**
Wen Jiabao **21, 42, 95**
White Dagoba (Jade Island,
    Beihai Park) **47**
Women's Street **53, 115**
World Trade Centre **64–5**

X/Y/Z

Xiangukou (Food) Street **55**
Xihai (West Lake) **45**
Yangmei Hutong **55**
Yaxiu Market **16**
Zhengyangmen ('Facing the
    Sun' Gate) **24**
Zhengyici Peking Opera
    Theatre **56**
Zhongnanhai (Beihai Park) **46**
Zhongshan Park **28**
Zhou Enlai **21**
Zongbu Hutong **66**